The darkness is past, and the true
light now shineth (1 John 2:8).

The Bug in the Ointment

The Bug in the Ointment

Understanding God's everlasting covenant through a survey of the historical background of the Biblical covenants.

Adrianne Asheburton

CFI Book Division
Gordonsville, Tennesee

Published by CFI Book Division

P.O. Box 159, Gordonsville, Tennessee 38563

Copyright © 2003, 2026 Adrianne Asheburton
978-0-9975122-7-4

Printed in the United States of America

Typeset in 11.5/13.8 Minion Pro

Note to the Reader

Night before last I was shown that evidences in regard to the covenants were clear and convincing. Yourself, Brother B, Brother C, and others are spending your investigative powers for naught to produce a position on the covenants to vary from the position that Brother [E.J.] Waggoner has presented. Had you received the true light which shineth, you would not have imitated or gone over the same manner of interpretation and misconstruing the Scriptures as did the Jews. What made them so zealous? Why did they hang on the words of Christ? Why did spies follow Him to mark His words that they could repeat and misinterpret and twist in a way to mean that which their own unsanctified minds would make them to mean? In this way, they deceived the people. They made false issues. They handled those things that they could make a means of clouding and misleading minds.

The covenant question is a clear question and would be received by every candid, unprejudiced mind, but I was brought where the Lord gave me an insight into this matter. You have turned from plain light because you were afraid that the law question in Galatians would have to be accepted. (Ellen G. White, Letter to Uriah Smith, March 8, 1890).

Since I made the statement last Sabbath that the view of the covenants as it had been taught by Brother Waggoner was truth, it seems that great relief has come to many minds. (Ellen G. White, Letter to W.C. White and wife, March 10, 1890).

Table of Contents

Introduction 11

Part I: Suzerain Covenant Defined 13

Suzerain Covenant History 15

Suzerain Covenant Formula 21

Correlation of the Suzerain Treaty to the Sinai Covenant . . 25

Part II: Israel and the Suzerain Covenant 29

God's Original Purpose for His People 31

Conversion at the Red Sea? 35

Their Journey Begins 37

Foundation for the Suzerain Covenant at Sinai 43

Placed Under the Law 49

God's Original Objective Thwarted 53

Suzerain Covenant Restated to Israel 59

New Testament Commentary on the Sinaitic Events 63

Persistence of the Suzerain Mind-set
Throughout Ancient Israel's History 71

Part III: Israel's Breach of the Covenant Contract 75

Covenants of Israel with Assyria 77

Contracts of Judah with Assyria and Chaldea 81

Desperate Attempts at Political Stability 85

Covenant Lawsuit Proclaimed 87

Part IV: God's Everlasting Covenant 95

Original Objective for the Exodus from Egypt 97

Royal Land Grant Treaty as the Formula for the
Everlasting Covenant 103

Legal Foundations for the Land Grant 111

Part V: Covenant of Grace 117

Land Grant Formula Defines Abrahamic
Covenant of Grace 119

Staking the Claim 125

Land Grant Defines the Everlasting Kingdom of David . . . 127

Part VI: Unilateral Gift from the King 131

Confirmation of the Covenant 133

It's All About Inheritance—by Faith in the Promise 139

Circumcision—an Amendment to
the Everlasting Covenant? 143

Part VII: Suzerain Treaty Contrasted with Royal Land Grant . 149

Hebrew Distinction Between Covenants 151

Part VIII: The Historic Position 155

Covenant Theology in America 157

E.J. Waggoner's View of the Everlasting Covenant 161

Part IX: Persistence of Old Covenant Thinking 179

An Illustration of the Tenaciousness of the
Old Covenant Attitude 181

Bibliography 191

Introduction

You might think the title, *The Bug in the Ointment,* is an odd name for a theological discussion of the Biblical covenants. Solomon tells us in Ecclesiastes 10:1, "Dead flies cause the ointment of the apothecary to send forth a stinking savour."

For centuries a "bug" has permeated all of Christendom skewing the understanding of righteousness by faith, giving off a nauseating stench. This persistent "bug" is a common misconception about God's everlasting covenant: Is God's promise to redeem sinners all encompassing or limited in some way? Is salvation from sin based upon a contractual agreement with God, or the promise of God to all humanity?

Our High Priest has the remedy for our confusion. In Revelation 3:18 our Lord Jesus Christ counsels His remnant church to buy of Him the untainted eyesalve (ointment) that will cure our spiritual blindness. Only by giving up our preconceived opinions can we know the truth. We must allow Christ to cure our blindness.

In response to information I heard at a seminar in 2003, the original manuscript for *The Bug in the Ointment:Understanding God's Everlasting Covenant* was written. At that time I had already been studying God's everlasting covenant for about 15 years. The speaker at the seminar introduced a term I had never heard before. God's everlasting covenant was likened to an ancient Middle Eastern form of covenant called the "suzerain contract." This stimulated me to do additional study into the possible similarities and contrasts between God's everlasting covenant and the suzerain contract.

With subsequent study I discovered that the covenant made at Sinai did seem to follow the suzerain contract form. The suzerain method of contract/covenant used in ancient times, beginning with the Hittites, was a contract between a powerful conquering nation and a nation subdued by war and treaty. This form of covenant primarily benefitted the conqueror, but there were also benefits to the vassal nation in the form of protection given in return for allegiance and service. For the vassal it was an "obey and live" contract. Any violation of the contract committed by the conquered nation was swiftly met with a covenant lawsuit and punishment by the suzerain.

The prevailing theory that the suzerain contract is equivalent to God's everlasting covenant is erroneous and misleading. While the suzerain contract formula appears to be the style used at Sinai, especially noted in the Deuteronomic record, it does not follow the pattern of the everlasting covenant given to Adam and reiterated to Abraham, Isaac, and Jacob. This study examines the history of the suzerain contract contrasting it with God's everlasting (or "new") covenant as shown in the Biblical record in both the Old and New Testaments.

Can we overcome our misunderstanding of this vital point?

Part I

Suzerain Covenant Defined

1

Suzerain Covenant History

The first covenant method to be examined is often referred to as a suzerain covenant, treaty, or contract. Briefly defined, the suzerain covenant established a relationship that otherwise did not naturally exist between two or more parties. The covenant stipulations were spoken or read before the parties and then sanctioned by the swearing of an oath of allegiance in a ceremony of ratification. Use of the word suzerain to specify this type of treaty is a relatively new idea, even though the process has been in existence for millennia.

"Suzerain" didn't enter the English language until 1807. In Gosselin's *Power of the Pope of the Middle Ages*, it is used to describe the position of the pope over his vassals concerning territorial lands: "They may hold it in peace, and maintain therein the pure Catholic faith, saving the rights of the suzerain lord [the pope] (1853)." According to the *Oxford English Dictionary*, the formal definition of suzerain is: "A feudal overlord. In recent use, with reference to international relations, a sovereign or a state having supremacy over another state which possesses its own ruler or government but cannot act as an independent power."

While the word itself is relatively new to the English language, the concept has been traced by archeologists to an ancient legal process used by the Hittites beginning c. 1400 BC. This form of foreign relations treaty was used to control the activities of conquered foes. Through contract, the vassal nations were bound to the suzerain nation or king who possessed absolute authority over the conquered nations. The word came into English usage during the time of Napoleon Bonaparte's subjugation of the European nations. It was later applied to the diplomatic relations between Britain and the South African Republic, and also to the agreements between Turkey and Bulgaria from 1878 to

1909. By the mid-twentieth century, the word had been dropped from use in diplomatic terminology.[1]

How did the word suzerain come to be used in relation to the Biblical covenants? In 1954 George E. Mendenhall (1916 – 2016)[2] published a series of articles in *The Biblical Archeologist* on the subject of the law and the covenant in Israel and the ancient Near East. His discussion centered on newly discovered archeological documents dating back to about 1400 BC which revealed techniques by which the great Mesopotamian cultures exercised their coercive power upon the communities within their domain. Mendenhall contended that these ancient documents provided the foundation for understanding the laws and covenants of the Bible.

The ancient Mesopotamian cultures believed it was the function of the king to maintain justice and protection of the community at large. In most pagan cultures, the king was viewed as either a god or an earthly extension of a god. "What this meant in practice is probably that the legal policies were determined by the king and therefore received divine sanction."[3] These "divine" edicts could not be overturned as long as the king was alive.[4] "The largest number of examples of the suzerain-vassal treaty—and the most complete—are to be found in the fourteenth and thirteenth century Hittite texts."[5] From his examination of the ancient documents, Mendenhall developed a basic six point formula defining the treaties the powerful Hittite kings made with their conquered foes.

Mendenhall had an agenda behind his discussion on the suzerain treaty formula. From the middle of the nineteenth century, the dominant higher critical view promoted through German theologians was that the books of the Pentateuch were the result of oral traditions written and edited over hundreds of years rather than being written by Moses during Israel's wilderness sojourn. This was naturally disturbing to the more conservative evangelical theologians because it undermined the divine authorship and inspiration of the Biblical canon.

---

1. Bryan A. Garner, ed., *Blacks Law Dictionary*, seventh edition (St. Paul: West Group, 1999).
2. George Emory Mendenhall was professor emeritus of ancient and Biblical studies at the University of Michigan from 1954 until his retirement in 1986.
3. George E. Mendenhall, *Law and Covenant in Israel and the Ancient Near East* (Pittsburgh: The Biblical Colloquium, 1955), p. 4.
4. For example, see Esther 3:8-15, 8:8; and Daniel 6:4-9, 12, 15.
5. LaSor, William Sanford, David Allan Hubbard, Frederic Wm. Bush, *Old Testament Survey* (Grand Rapids, Mich.: Eerdmans, 1996), pp. 73-74.

Through the works of Julius Wellhausen (1844-1919), and later through Walter Eichrodt, J.G. Eichhorn, Rudolf Bultmann and others, this new source criticism view of the Pentateuch became a dominant theological opinion which crept into the writings of many prominent evangelical theologians.[6] From Genesis, Wellhausen dissected what he claimed was two distinct narrative structures, identifying them with the use of two names for God—Yahweh and Elohim. His determination was that these narratives were the oldest portion of the Pentateuch, while the laws and rituals of Exodus and Deuteronomy were elements that had been edited in and were from a much later period in Israelite history.

Wellhausen claimed that these characteristics evolved over a long period of time beginning with ancient Israel's early nomadic religion, continuing through the settlement period, and then to the formal giving of the law at about the time of the major prophets (seventh century BC). Wellhausen believed "Moses the law-giver at Sinai, through whom God gave to Israel the extensive and minute legislation of the theocratic community, is but the fictitious creation of much later periods, beginning in the writings of J [Yahweh/Jehovah] and E [Elohim], developing through the work of the redactor who combined these two documents (the Jehovist) and the book of Deuteronomy, and finding its culmination in the Priestly presentation of the Sinai events."[7] Thus, according to Wellhausen and other higher critics, the writing of the Pentateuch took place over about seven centuries, instead of being written by Moses during the forty years of wilderness wandering. This was contrary to the traditional view on the writing of the Pentateuch, which followed the chronological format of the narrative structures presented in the Old Testament canon.

Wellhausen's presentation of the Israelite religion declared that the development of a covenant between God and Israel was the result of the preaching of the later prophets rather than being given through Moses at Sinai, pushing the date forward to the time of Jeremiah.[8] Because of the emphasis of the eighth-century prophets (BC) on God's righteousness and His demand for social justice, Wellhausen claimed this as evidence for a shift "from a covenant as a natural bond [like that of a father and a son] to one of a pact or treaty. Commandments were understood as

---

6. See, for example, the *International Critical Commentary on Genesis* authored by John Skinner, first published in 1910.

7. Ernest W. Nicholson, *God and His People* (Oxford, England: Clarendon Press, 1986), p. 4.

8. Jeremiah 11:1-10.

demands or conditions on which Yahweh's continued relation to Israel depended. The natural bond between Yahweh and Israel was severed. Many scholars accepted Wellhausen's covenant ideas and considered the issue settled. There was little debate among the scholars on the covenant for a while."[9]

Mendenhall sought a means by which he could counteract the reconstruction of the history of Israel's religion. The discovery of the Hittite treaty documents provided him with this tool. Mendenhall's agenda was an attempt to rescue the historical validity of the Biblical record from the higher critical attacks of Wellhausen's theory of multiple authorship of the Pentateuch.

By showing that the suzerain treaty formula was the foundation of the covenant God made with Israel at Sinai, Mendenhall provided evidence for a fifteenth century BC authorship of the Pentateuch. Mendenhall "argued that the Hittite treaty was an early source of the Old Testament's idea of covenant. [He] argued that the tribes of Israel were not bound together by blood-ties but by a covenant based on religion and modeled after the suzerainty treaty by which the great Hittite king bound his vassals to faithfulness and obedience to himself."[10]

Believing that all religion is based on covenant, Mendenhall claimed that "a study of the covenant form as we know it in ancient legal documents may possibly serve to bring into the chaos of opinion some objective criteria for reconstructing the course of Israelite history and religion."[11]

Meredith G. Kline, establishing his thesis on Mendenhall's studies, maintained that "The origin of the Old Testament canon coincided with the founding of the kingdom of Israel by covenant at Sinai. The very treaty that formally established the Israelite theocracy was itself the beginning and the nucleus of the total covenantal cluster of writings which constitutes the Old Testament canon."

Kline's insistence that the suzerain treaty formula was the foundation of the covenant God made with Israel was, like Mendenhall, centered on combating the higher critical view of the Pentateuch. "Our conclusion in a word, then, is that canon is inherent in covenant, covenant of the kind attested in ancient international relations and the Mosaic covenants of

---

9. Ralph L. Smith, *Old Testament Theology* (Nashville, Tenn.: Broadman & Holman, 1993), p. 139.
10. Ibid., p. 140.
11. Mendenhall, p. 24.

the Bible. Hence it is to this covenant structure that theology should turn for its perspective and model in order to articulate its doctrine of canon in terms historically concrete and authentic. It is the covenant form that will explain the particular historical-legal traits of the divine authority that confronts us in the Scriptures."[12]

---

12. Meredith G. Kline, *The Structure of Biblical Authority* (Eugene, Ore.: Wipf and Stock Publishers, 1997), pp. 43-44.

2

Suzerain Covenant Formula

In his articles, Mendenhall advanced his view that the Sinaitic covenant had a definite historical setting and he used the dates for the newly discovered Hittite treaties as the foundational support for his theory. Mendenhall argued that the Hittite treaty formula was used by God to define the covenant made with Israel at Sinai. He felt that the Hittite covenant was familiar to Moses and the children of Israel, and could have been appropriately used by God at Sinai to express His plans to them.

By analyzing the suzerainty treaty documents, he found an amazing correlation between the secular documents and the Sinai covenant tradition as written by Moses (Exodus chapters 19–24 and the whole of Deuteronomy, especially, the blessings and curses in chapters 27–29). If the Israelite covenant could be shown to be based on the Hittite suzerainty treaty form which was known to exist between c. 1400–1200 BC, then Wellhausen's position that the Pentateuch was written over a seven hundred year period could more easily be refuted. Comprehending the underlying agenda of Mendenhall's study determines his focus, and reveals the theological environment which allowed and influenced the advancement of the secular suzerain covenant theory as the method for the covenant God made with ancient Israel at Sinai.

Examining the various instances of covenant language throughout the Bible, Mendenhall determined there was considerable variation in the order of the elements, the wording of the elements, and that some of the elements occasionally were not included. Working from the ancient Hittite tablets, Mendenhall identified six main elements to the suzerain treaty method and included three more elements as conclusionary components. We will list the elements and then describe them more fully.

1. Preamble
2. Historical prologue
3. Stipulations
4. Provision for deposition and periodic reading of the covenant
5. List of witnesses
6. Blessings and curses
7. A formal oath on the part of the vassal
8. Solemn ceremony (see Exodus 24:9–11 for God's use of this ceremony)
9. Formulation for initiating action against the rebellious vassal (guidelines for the lawsuit)

In the preamble the author of the document is identified, giving his title, territory, attributes, and his genealogy. The emphasis was always on the majesty and power of the sovereign (suzerain). In ancient pagan cultures that used the suzerain treaty pattern, the suzerain was often thought of as a god who was writing his treaty to confer a covenantal relationship upon his vassals.

The historical prologue described in detail the circumstances of the previous relations between the two parties, listing the many great things the suzerain king had performed for the benefit of the vassal. Forming an essential element, the historical prologue was always found in the completely preserved Hittite documents. This section of the document was never stereotyped or impersonal, but rather listed specific descriptions of actual historical events that had taken place between the king and the vassal. Mendenhall stressed "it is most important to see that the vassal is *exchanging* future obedience to specific commands for past benefits which he received without any real right."[1] Since the Hittite king was the author of the document, he spoke in the first person directly to the vassal in an "I—thou" form of address, indicating the personal and benevolent relationship between the king and vassal.

The third part of the treaty was the stipulations. The stipulations and obligations were varied depending on the situation with the conquered kingdoms, the condition of the vassal nations, and the whim of the suzerain. However, Mendenhall discovered several stipulation elements usually occurring in the documents.

---

1. Mendenhall, p. 32; emphasis in original.

These included:—

1. The prohibition of an alliance with any other foreign nation outside the Hittite empire.
2. The payment of taxes to the suzerain lord.
3. Prohibition of enmity against anything the Hittite suzerain decreed.
4. The demand that the vassal nation answer a call to arms when the suzerain was planning war against another nation.
5. The vassal was to guard the edges of the suzerain's domain, being watchful for any invasion of foreign armies or spies.
6. The vassal king must hold enduring and unbounded trust in the suzerain's ability to rule. It was forbidden for a vassal to entertain any malicious rumor about the suzerain, or speak any evil words against him. To do so was interpreted as the beginning of rebellion.
7. The vassal was forbidden to give asylum to refugees from any source because these might be construed as foreign instigators or insurrectionists and therefore dangerous to the suzerain's absolute rule. Extradition of criminals was expected.
8. The vassal must appear before the Hittite king at least once a year bringing tribute (taxes, see for example Esther 1:1–5).
9. Any controversies between co-vassals in the suzerain's kingdom were to be brought before the suzerain for judgment. The suzerain was sole judge of his realm.

It is clear from reading these stipulations that the suzerain intended to maintain not only a dominating position over his vassal lords and their nations, but also to maintain peace between the vassals themselves. Therefore the stipulations could be said to relate partly to the sovereign and partly to the residents of the suzerain's domain.

Provision for the deposition of the document in the temple of the chief god, and the specification that the document was to be read aloud before the people on a periodic basis, ensured that the people would be reminded continually of their obligations to the sovereign. "Since it was not only the vassal king, but his entire state which was bound by the treaty, periodic public reading served a double purpose: first, to familiarize the entire populace with the obligations to the great king; and second, to increase respect for the vassal king by describing the close and warm relationship [he had] with the mighty and majestic Emperor."[2] By being deposited in the sacred temple, it imposed the idea that the treaty itself was under the protection of the deity and could not be breached without bringing the wrath of the deity upon the people.

Just as legal documents today are witnessed by a notary, judge, or other official of the community, the Hittite documents were attested to by the gods of the realm. "This section enumerates the deities who are invoked, usually a considerable number. Included are, of course, the gods of the Hittite state, but the pantheon of the vassal state is also included. In other words, the gods of the vassals themselves enforce the covenant."[3] Mendenhall noted that the deified mountains, rivers, springs, sea, heaven and earth were also included in the list of witnesses. In comparing the suzerain treaty to the Biblical covenant, he correlated the calling of nature as "witnesses" with Isaiah 1:2 and Deuteronomy 32:1. (See also Deuteronomy 4:26; 30:19).

Though it was a secular and political document, the suzerain treaty was couched in religious terms. The blessings and curses included as part of the document indicated the divine beneficence or wrath that would be invoked upon the vassal for his behavior—whether obedience or disobedience. It was a faithless covenant based on fear, not faith. Even though it was the Hittite king who would proceed with military force against the rebellious vassal, the idea was conveyed that the king was acting as an agent of the provoked deity. Mendenhall and Kline both see parallels between the suzerain treaty and the blessings and curses found in Deuteronomy 28.

Because they took place during a formal ceremony, the final elements of the suzerain formula can all be packaged together. These included the ratification of the treaty by the recitation of a formal oath on the part of the vassal pledging his complete obedience to the sovereign. This was followed by a solemn ceremony which included sacrifices and feasts. Mendenhall insisted also that "it is quite likely that some form existed for initiating procedure against a rebellious vassal"[4] to bring a covenant lawsuit for violation of the stipulations. Thus Mendenhall concluded a total of nine elements in the Hittite covenant formula.

––––––––––––––

2. Ibid., p. 34.
3. Ibid., p. 34.
4. Ibid., p. 35.

3

Correlation of the Suzerain Treaty to the Sinai Covenant

Many detailed studies have been done correlating the elements of the suzerain treaty to the Biblical traditions of the covenant at Sinai as recorded in Exodus and Deuteronomy. Exodus chapters 19 to 24 and the whole of Deuteronomy follow the suzerain pattern. Kline saw the "aptness of the broad identification of the pre-Messianic Scriptures as 'the covenant' or 'the old covenant'" by describing God as Israel's heavenly King and Israel as God's vassal people. "For all Israel's life, cult, culture … stood under the covenant rule of Yahweh. A peculiar significance was imparted to the whole by Yahweh's presence in the midst as God-King. His covenantal dominion, exercised from the nation's cultic center, the royal site of the theophanic presence, claimed Israel's life to its full circumference."[1]

Suzerain treaty expressions are noted by many theologians in the giving of the law in Exodus chapters 20 to 23 and in Deuteronomy. "In the ancient world, relationships between individuals as well as between states were ordered and regulated by means of covenants, or treaties. Numerous examples of such instruments of international diplomacy have survived, deriving from various parts of the ancient Near East. These divide into two basic categories: (1) a parity treaty, where the contracting parties negotiate as equals, and (2) a suzerain-vassal treaty, where one party transparently imposes its will on the other. A study of these documents, particularly those of the later type, leaves no doubt as to the influence of the ancient Near Eastern treaty patterns on the external, formal, literary aspects of the biblical *berit*. The affinities are to be expected. In order for the *berit* to be intelligible to the Israelites, it

---

1. Kline, p. 46.

made sense to structure it according to the accepted patterns of the then universally recognized legal instruments."[2]

Relying on statements from the Scripture itself, Kline states, "The laws recorded in Exodus 20:22–23:33 are specifically identified as 'the book of the covenant' (Exod. 24:7; cf. 4). The fact that this covenantal collection of laws deals with matters moral and ceremonial, civil and cultic, individual and corporate, is indicative of how all Israel's life fell within the purview and under the regulation of Yahweh's covenant with them."[3] Kline claimed that the suzerain contract made at Sinai specifically dealt with the nation of Israel, and with the laws regulating Israel's conduct both toward God in religious matters and toward fellow men in civil matters. Following Mendenhall's lead, Kline claimed that the formula for this covenant was found in the ancient international suzerain treaties.

Proving his position by elaborating on the points Mendenhall developed, Kline finds correlation to the suzerain form in several sections of Scripture (in its broadest context, Kline claims that the whole of the Old Testament follows the suzerain covenant pattern).[4] Specifically, the giving of the Decalogue and the entire book of Deuteronomy are seen by Kline as following the suzerain treaty contract form. "The pattern of the suzerainty treaty can be traced in miniature in the revelation written on the tables by the finger of God." "Deuteronomy is precisely the treaty document given by Yahweh through Moses to be the canonical foundation of Israel's life in covenant relationship with himself."[5]

At Sinai, Moses was instructed to prepare the people for their face to face encounter with their Suzerain Lord (Exodus 19:10, 11). The preamble of the suzerain treaty is clearly stated in Exodus 20:2, and restated in Deuteronomy 5:6. "I am the LORD thy God." Yahweh, the self-existent One, is God. The historical prologue follows immediately after this: "… which have brought thee out of the land of Egypt, out of the house of bondage" (Exodus 20:2; and Deuteronomy 1:9–4:20, which gives an extended history for obvious reasons). In these statements God declares Himself to be the only one responsible for their deliverance from Egyptian slavery, and for sustaining and protecting them during their wilderness journey. No one else could make this claim. God placed

---

2. Nahum M. Sarna, *Exodus, The JPS Torah Commentary* (New York: Jewish Publication Society, 1991), p. 102.
3. Kline, pp. 48-49.
4. Ibid., pp. 48-75; 113-130.
5. Ibid., pp. 114, 56.

Himself before the Israelites as their only Saviour and Lord to whom they owed their very existence and safety.

Next, according to Kline, follows the stipulations of the contract (Exodus 20:3–17 and Deuteronomy 5:7–21). As God's vassals, the corporate nation of Israel and, individually the people, were forbidden from forming an alliance with any foreign deity. Enmity against the true God or showing disrespect for their Suzerain, was also forbidden. Lack of respect indicated a rebellious attitude the Suzerain would not tolerate. God knew that fraternizing with ideas and material things of the foreign nations would turn the minds of the people away from Him, so He included stipulations regarding just these situations. Paralleling the requirement of the vassal to appear before the Suzerain on a regular basis, we find the Decalogue stipulates that each week the vassal was to appear before God to hear the reading of the words of the covenant, thereby showing an enduring confidence in the Suzerain as their Lord and Master. It was understood that the word of the Sovereign Lord and Master could not be changed in any way. Tribute was also defined by Kline as taking the form of tithes and offerings, and sacrifices as set forth in the ceremonial laws.

The commandments regulating man's conduct with his fellow man follow the format of the suzerain treaty as the reigning Monarch detailed specifics for His people's civil and social interactions (Exodus 21:1–23:33; Deuteronomy 6:1–25; 12:1–26:1–19). Blessings for obedience and curses for disobedience are expounded in detail in Deuteronomy chapters 27 through 30. It is important to note that unlike the Hittite suzerain contracts where blessings and curses fell on both parties, "The covenant of Moses, on the other hand is almost the exact opposite. It imposes specific obligations upon the tribes or clans without binding Yahweh to specific obligations, though it goes without saying that the covenant relationship itself presupposed the protection and support of Yahweh to Israel."[6]

Continuing with Kline's premise, the contract was ratified at Sinai through the blood of the sacrifice which was sprinkled on the people (Exodus 24:5–8) to purify and sanctify them. Then God called Moses, the priests, and the elders as representatives of the people to come up into the Mount for a covenantal meal (Exodus 24:9–11). During this event the selected men, corporate representatives of the vassal nation, were witnesses to the power and majesty of their Sovereign. Pertinent Biblical

---

6. Mendenhall, p. 36.

parallels give definition from the perspective of a political suzerainty, as for example the feast given by Ahasuerus for his vassals (Esther 1:1–9) and Nebuchadnezzar's festival of the golden image (Daniel 3:2, 3).

From these parallels it seems clear that the suzerain treaty formula was used by God when He gave His covenant to the children of Israel at Sinai. "All these elements in the traditions of Israel hold together and indeed make sense only on the supposition that there actually was a covenant relation as the basis of the system. The federation itself is almost certainly an adaptation of political devises which had been used by the peoples of Palestine and Syria for centuries before. It was the only way in which small political groups could have any hope at all for self-determination in the face of much more powerful enemies."[7] As the children of Israel were about to enter a land resistant and hostile to their takeover of the territory, they would certainly need the protection of a powerful Suzerain on their side.

---

7. Ibid., p. 37.

Part II

Israel and the Suzerain Covenant

4

God's Original Purpose
for His People

When the children of Israel were assembled at the foot of Mount Sinai, God called Moses up into the mountain to give him instructions for His people. The instructions were fundamental for their daily lives and simple to comprehend.

And Moses went up unto God, and the Lord called unto him out of the mountain, saying, Thus shalt thou say to the house of Jacob, and tell the children of Israel; Ye have seen what I did unto the Egyptians, and how I bare you on eagles' wings, and brought you unto Myself. Now therefore, if ye will obey My voice indeed, and keep My covenant, then ye shall be a peculiar treasure unto Me above all people: for all the earth is Mine: and ye shall be unto Me a kingdom of priests, and an holy nation. These are the words which thou shalt speak unto the children of Israel (Exodus 19:3–6).

The Lord was simply saying: "Moses, tell My people that if they will remember how I have taken care of them in the past, then they will have faith in Me and know that I will continue to deliver and protect them. If they will listen to My proclamation and cherish My promise that I gave to their fathers Abraham, Isaac, and Jacob, I promise them now that they will be My peculiar treasure, a kingdom of ambassadors who will declare My truths throughout all the earth, a sanctified and separate people, dedicated to My ways."

This instruction is unrhetorical, to the point, and easy to understand. God did not intend for His Gospel to be difficult or burdensome. In these words from the Lord, there are no curses, only blessings, and the blessings would come through the hearing of faith which remembers

God's power to deliver His people from all adversity and preserve them as a holy people, consecrated to Him and His work.

How did we get from these few verses that are so full of promise and blessing, to the suzerain contract formula that followed only a few short chapters later? Why did the people feel the need to promise God anything in return? Why does God seem to change His method (or did He change His method?) for dealing with His people? Was it God's original plan that His people would view Him as a demanding Suzerain who would rule them with an iron hand? A review of the events leading up to Sinai will help us better comprehend the situation.

The Call from Bondage

Moses told Pharaoh that he was to release the children of Israel from their bondage so that they could worship their God in the desert. Moses and Aaron confronted Pharaoh, speaking the words of God to him:

> Thus saith the LORD God of Israel, "Let My people go, that they may hold a feast unto Me in the wilderness. … The God of the Hebrews hath met with us: let us go, we pray thee, three days' journey into the desert, and sacrifice unto the LORD our God; lest He fall upon us with pestilence, or with the sword." In his pride and arrogance Pharaoh retorted, "Who is the LORD, that I should obey His voice to let Israel go? I know not the LORD, neither will I let Israel go" (Exodus 5:1–3).

Thus begins a back and forth struggle between Pharaoh and God resulting in ten plagues, including the death of the first born of all creatures, and the destruction of the Egyptian army. Our reason for mentioning this section of Scripture is not because we need a review of its history, but to examine the apparent disjunction between what was said and what actually occurred. There was an inconsistency between what Moses told Pharaoh about the length of the journey and the actual time it took the Israelites to get to Mount Sinai. Why did a three day journey into the desert end up taking seven weeks to reach the destination? Understanding this will assist our comprehension of the monumental problem God was facing in His effort to free His people from their slave mentality.[1] Between Egypt and Mount Sinai we find a chiastic sequence of events which yields great insight into the spiritual condition of the children of Israel.

---

1. I am indebted to Robert Van Ornam for this turn of phrase.

The children of Israel needed a radical new way of thinking about God and themselves as His special people.[2] Not only were the people enslaved physically by Egypt's mastery over their bodies, but they were mentally captivated as well by Egypt's myriad spiritual deceptions. Their slave mentality had to be transformed. They needed to know they could freely choose whom they would serve.

> It is extremely difficult for a slave, even after having gained his freedom, to act or think like a free man. ... The strain of their prolonged bondage and the fatigue of their daily routine had drained them of all spirituality. Specifically because of this bondage—Bnei Yisrael had grown instinctively dependent upon their Egyptian masters. Therefore, to facilitate their transformation—from Pharaoh's slaves to God's servants—they must change their instinctive physical dependence on Egypt to a cognitive spiritual dependence on God.[3]

This was going to prove a difficult lesson for them to learn.

---

2. Compare: Exodus 14:5-10; 15:22-26; 16:1-3; 17:1-3; and 17:8-16. The chiastic structure is war, water, food, water, war. Each trial was intended to bring Israel to a true perception of their helplessness and shift their dependence from Egypt and self to the benevolent power of God, who alone was able to deliver them and provide for their every need.

3. Rabbi Menachem Leibtag, "Parshat Beshalach—A Desert Seminar"; Internet article found at: http://www.tanach.org/shmot/bshal1.htm

5

Conversion at the Red Sea?

Why did God lead the tribes of Israel in the circuitous route that resulted in them being trapped between the Egyptian army and the waters of the Red Sea? What was God's purpose? If His purpose had been the destruction of the Egyptians, He could have accomplished that during the plagues. God had to bring the people to the place where, with death in front and behind, there was no other option except entire dependence upon God for their deliverance. Their reaction to this traumatic situation reveals the true condition of their heart.

> And they said unto Moses, because there were no graves in Egypt, hast thou taken us away to die in the wilderness? wherefore hast thou dealt thus with us, to carry us forth out of Egypt? Is not this the word that we did tell thee in Egypt, saying, let us alone, that we may serve the Egyptians? For it had been better for us to serve the Egyptians, than that we should die in the wilderness (Exodus 14:11, 12).

These words, spoken in fear, were an indictment against God's credibility and competence as their Leader. God responds to this unwarranted complaint against His power to deliver them by commanding them to "fear not, stand still, and see the salvation of the Lord ... for the Egyptians whom ye have seen today, ye shall see them again no more forever" (Exodus 14:13). While this verse appears to be a promise, deeper examination of the intent of the Hebrew words proves it is actually a command. According to the Talmud "God here does not promise His nation that they will never face an Egyptian army again [we know from Scripture that they did]. Rather, He commands them to 'never again' look to Egypt for their salvation."[1]

---

1. Liebtag, Ibid.

God was inviting the slaves of Pharaoh to realize the profound freedom they could have if they would turn their affections and allegiance from Egypt to God. Centuries later, Ezekiel remembers Israel's high calling and command to forsake all of Egypt's enticements:—

> In the day when I chose Israel, and lifted up Mine hand unto the seed of the house of Jacob, and made Myself known unto them in the land of Egypt, when I lifted up Mine hand unto them, saying, I am the LORD your God; in the day that I lifted up Mine hand unto them, to bring them forth of the land of Egypt into a land that I had espied for them, flowing with milk and honey, which is the glory of all lands: then said I unto them, Cast ye away every man the abominations of his eyes, and defile not yourselves with the idols of Egypt: I am the LORD your God.

When Ezekiel wrote his words nine centuries after the exodus, the children of Israel had never learned this simple lesson:—

> But they rebelled against Me, and would not hearken unto Me: they did not every man cast away the abominations of their eyes, neither did they forsake the idols of Egypt (Ezekiel 20:5–8).

6

Their Journey Begins

There was only one reason God delivered the Israelites from Egypt: to fulfill His oath to Abraham, which would vindicate His holy name, teaching the people that He alone was worthy of worship. He alone was their true covenant-keeping sovereign Lord and Master.

But I wrought for My name's sake, that it should not be polluted before the heathen, among whom they were, in whose sight I made myself known unto them, in bringing them forth out of the land of Egypt. Wherefore I caused them to go forth out of the land of Egypt, and brought them into the wilderness. And I gave them My statutes, and shewed them My judgments, which if a man do, he shall even live in them.

Moreover also I gave them My Sabbaths, to be a sign between Me and them, that they might know that I am the LORD that sanctify them. But the house of Israel rebelled against Me in the wilderness: they walked not in My statutes, and they despised My judgments, which if a man do, he shall even live in them; and My Sabbaths they greatly polluted: then I said, I would pour out My fury upon them in the wilderness, to consume them. But I wrought for My name's sake, that it should not be polluted before the heathen, in whose sight I brought them out.

Yet also I lifted up My hand unto them in the wilderness, that I would not bring them into the land which I had given them, flowing with milk and honey, which is the glory of all lands; because they despised My judgments, and walked not in My statutes, but polluted My Sabbaths: for their heart went after their idols.

Nevertheless Mine eye spared them from destroying them, neither did I make an end of them in the wilderness. But I said unto their children in the wilderness, Walk ye not in the statutes of your fathers, neither observe their judgments, nor defile yourselves with their idols: I am the LORD your God; walk in My statutes, and keep My judgments, and do them; and hallow My Sabbaths; and they shall be a sign between Me and you, that ye may know that I am the LORD your God.

Notwithstanding the children rebelled against Me: they walked not in My statutes, neither kept My judgments to do them, which if a man do, he shall even live in them; they polluted My Sabbaths: then I said, I would pour out My fury upon them, to accomplish My anger against them in the wilderness.

Nevertheless I withdrew Mine hand, and wrought for My name's sake, that it should not be polluted in the sight of the heathen, in whose sight I brought them forth. I lifted up Mine hand unto them also in the wilderness, that I would scatter them among the heathen, and disperse them through the countries; because they had not executed My judgments, but had despised My statutes, and had polluted My Sabbaths, and their eyes were after their fathers' idols.

Wherefore I gave them also statutes that were not good, and judgments whereby they should not live; and I polluted them in their own gifts, in that they caused to pass through the fire all that openeth the womb, that I might make them desolate, to the end that they might know that I am the LORD.

Therefore, son of man, speak unto the house of Israel, and say unto them, Thus saith the Lord GOD; Yet in this your fathers have blasphemed Me, in that they have committed a trespass against Me. For when I had brought them into the land, for the which I lifted up Mine hand to give it to them, then they saw every high hill, and all the thick trees, and they offered there their sacrifices, and there they presented the provocation of their offering: there also they made their sweet savour, and poured out there their drink offerings.

Then I said unto them, What is the high place whereunto ye go? And the name thereof is called Bamah unto this day. Wherefore say unto the house of Israel, Thus saith the Lord GOD; Are ye polluted after the manner of your fathers? and commit ye whoredom after their abominations? For when ye offer your gifts, when ye make your sons to pass through the fire, ye pollute yourselves with all your idols, even unto this day: and shall I be enquired of by you, O house of Israel?

As I live, saith the Lord GOD, I will not be enquired of by you. And that which cometh into your mind shall not be at all, that ye say, We will be as the heathen, as the families of the countries, to serve wood and stone.

As I live, saith the Lord GOD, surely with a mighty hand, and with a stretched out arm, and with fury poured out, will I rule over you: and I will bring you out from the people, and will gather you out of the countries wherein ye are scattered, with a mighty hand, and with a stretched out arm, and with fury poured out. And I will bring you into the wilderness of the people, and there will I plead with you face to face. Like as I pleaded with your fathers in the wilderness of the land of Egypt, so will I plead with you, saith the Lord GOD.

And I will cause you to pass under the rod, and I will bring you into the bond of the covenant: and I will purge out from among you the rebels, and them that transgress against Me: I will bring them forth out of the country where they sojourn, and they shall not enter into the land of Israel: and ye shall know that I am the LORD.

As for you, O house of Israel, thus saith the Lord GOD; Go ye, serve ye every one his idols, and hereafter also, if ye will not hearken unto Me: but pollute ye My holy name no more with your gifts, and with your idols. For in Mine holy mountain, in the mountain of the height of Israel, saith the Lord GOD, there shall all the house of Israel, all of them in the land, serve Me: there will I accept them, and there will I require your offerings, and the firstfruits of your oblations, with all your holy things. I will accept you with your sweet savour, when I bring you out from the people, and gather you out of the countries wherein ye have been scattered; and I will be sanctified in you before the heathen.

And ye shall know that I am the LORD, when I shall bring you into the land of Israel, into the country for the which I lifted up Mine hand to give it to your fathers. And there shall ye remember your ways, and all your doings, wherein ye have been defiled; and ye shall lothe yourselves in your own sight for all your evils that ye have committed. And ye shall know that I am the LORD, when I have wrought with you for My name's sake, not according to your wicked ways, nor according to your corrupt doings, O ye house of Israel, saith the Lord GOD. (Ezekiel 20:9-44).

Relief from the strain of facing certain destruction brought shouts of joy and celebration when all the people were assembled on the eastern bank of the Red Sea. Delivery seemingly produced the "correct" response from God's chosen people and they spontaneously broke out in the singing of praises. (see Exodus 15:1).

Having crossed the Red Sea on dry ground and celebrated their freedom with a victory song, the children of Israel began their journey to meet their God. As the liberated nation of slaves ventured deeper into the desert, they encountered various difficulties. For many years they had been slaves to a dominating, demanding suzerain who severely punished them for any infraction of his decrees. Their mind was thoroughly bent in a slave mentality that could hardly imagine the meaning of freedom. Now as they wandered farther out into unknown territory, they began to doubt the promise of freedom proclaimed to them by God through Moses. Yes, they had miraculously escaped the horrors of the plagues, and the death threats of Pharaoh, but it seemed to them that it was only to face death by dehydration and starvation in the hot, sandy barrenness of the Sinai desert. To these barely liberated slaves, it seemed they had only traded one despot for another, so blind were they to the true character of God.

Their lack of faith in God's promises displays itself after only three days, when they arrive at Marah finding the water poisonous. Through a miracle, the water is made pure. This was their first test of faith which they failed because they forgot all the blessings they had previously received from God's hand. Because of their lack of faith, God informed them that the only way they could survive was to "diligently harken" to His voice (Exodus 15:26). Here, near the shore of the Red Sea, God counseled them to listen to His commandments and His statutes (the ones already in existence). If they could exhibit even this small amount of faith, they would begin to find on every hand blessings instead of curses.

From Marah they move on, coming to the Wilderness of Zin where they once again sin against their Lord, accusing Him of bringing them into the wilderness to kill them. Moses warned them of their rebellious attitude: "Your murmurings are not against us, but against the LORD" (Exodus 16:8). Again, the people fail the test of faith. And again, instead of punishing them for their doubting, rebellious attitude God blessed them with "angel's bread" from heaven; food rained abundantly from the skies. Two beneficent miracles performed when, according to their slave mentality, they should have received curses and punishment for their querulousness toward their new Suzerain.

Pushing on toward their destination deep in the heart of the Sinai desert, the children of Israel come to Rephidim. Months of loving, personal attention from their Lord and Master have by this time taken place. Every day He blessed them with all they needed, even providing a cloud over their head to protect them from the blazing heat of the desert sun, and a pillar of fire at night to protect them from the night chill, yet they persisted in their unbelief. At Rephidim they stumble and fall over the same test regarding drinking water. Their refusal to heed God's counsel about "remembering" caused them to repeat their sin against their Master. Persistent unbelief would be their downfall (Hebrews 3:17–19; 4:1–3).

Not only were these lessons designed to teach them about their physical dependence upon God, but their spiritual dependence was also brought home to them in the Sabbath rest (Exodus 16:22–26; Hebrews 4:2–6). Three trials and three failures on the part of the children of Israel. The lesson God intended to teach His people was that they were to give up dependence upon Egypt (as a symbol of sin and self) and recognize God for who He really is, the great I AM. This fundamental truth was never actualized in their lives.

7

Foundation for the Suzerain Covenant at Sinai

Three months after departing Egypt and their slavery to Pharaoh, the children of Israel arrived at Sinai, the place where they would meet their Sovereign Lord face to face. God spoke to Moses, telling him to remind the people again that if only they would remember all that He had done for them in the past (going all the way back to the call of Abraham, their father) they would find faith, allowing God to perfect their characters. He promised to make them a "kingdom of priests, and an holy nation" (Exodus 19:3–6). Remembering all God has previously done for us builds faith in His future protection and blessings, developing confident dependence upon His power to save us from sin.

When Moses brought these glad tidings down from the mountaintop to the people, in their persistent unbelief in God's power and lack of knowledge of His true character, they made an impetuous response.

> Moses returned to the camp, and having summoned the elders of Israel, he repeated to them the divine message. Their answer was, "All that the Lord hath spoken we will do." Thus they entered into a solemn covenant with God, pledging themselves to accept Him as their ruler, by which they became, in a special sense, the subjects of His authority.[1]

The promise of the people to meet the stipulations of what they supposed was an offer of a treaty between themselves and their Suzerain, was presumptuously declared by them even before they heard the conditions of the covenant (Exodus 19:8). The *wording* of the response was not wrong, with the exception that those words were grounded in fear, not faith.

---

1. Ellen G. White, *Patriarchs and Prophets*, p. 303.

And Moses came, and called for the elders of the people, and laid before their faces all these words which the Lord commanded him. And all the people answered together, and said, All that the Lord hath spoken we will do. This is the pledge that God's people are to make in these last days. Their acceptance with God depends on a faithful fulfilment of the terms of their agreement with Him. God included in His covenant all who will obey Him. To all who will do justice and judgment, keeping their hand from doing any evil, the promise is, Even to them will I give in Mine house and within My walls a place and a name better than of sons and daughters; I will give them an everlasting name, that shall not be cut off.[2]

There is nothing inherently wrong with giving our pledge of allegiance to God, provided the heart is fully converted and knows its complete dependence upon our Sovereign Lord—that He will fulfill His oath to us to redeem us from all sin and restore us as His children and rightful heirs to His kingdom (Genesis 15:17, 18; Hebrews 6:16–18). Our honest, heart-felt pledge of allegiance fulfills the first three commandments. From that naturally flows obedience to the other seven as the converted heart determines, like Joseph, to never do anything that will insult our Sovereign Lord (Genesis 39:9).

From this pledge of allegiance to God will arise the justice and judgment toward others that fulfills all righteousness. When true allegiance results from a heart-felt appreciation of God's gift of salvation from sin, it will result in a code of conduct which exhibits that appreciation. Such was not the case with the children of Israel at Sinai, and never was the case with them all through their experience right up to the time of Christ and onward. It was their old covenant self-dependence that caused them to reject the Lord's continuous pleas for repentance, which finally led them to crucify their Redeemer.

What was God's response to their promise? Forty years later, as Moses rehearsed the history of Sinai to the children, he informs us of God's response to their impetuous promise. "And the LORD heard the voice of your words, when ye spake unto me; and the LORD said unto me, I have heard the voice of the words of this people, which they have spoken unto thee: they have well said all that they have spoken. *O that there were such an heart in them*, that they would fear Me, and keep all My commandments always, that it might be well with them, and with their

____

2. Ellen G. White, Letter 263, 1903; see also Revelation 2:17; 3:12.

children for ever!" (Deuteronomy 5:28, 29). In His divine foreknowledge He looked down through the coming centuries and sadly said, "*O, that this would be true!!*" (Matthew 23:34–38; Revelation 3:14–22).

He knew their promise was based on their unstable characters and was stated without true faith in His power to deliver them. It indicated that the people were so full of pride in themselves that they couldn't see their abysmal impotence in meeting any demands from their Sovereign Lord. If their pledge had been one of allegiance offered from a humbled heart that knew its complete dependence upon God for every strength needed to obey, the pledge would have then been acceptable to God. However, it was not so with the unconverted Israelites. Their pledge was an old covenant promise, based in pride and self-sufficiency, which necessitated that God bring them under law until they learned their true condition.

> There is no safety nor repose nor justification in transgression of the law. Man cannot hope to stand innocent before God, and at peace with Him through the merits of Christ, while he continues in sin. He must cease to transgress, and become loyal and true. As the sinner looks into the great moral looking glass, he sees his defects of character. He sees himself just as he is, spotted, defiled, and condemned. But he knows that the law cannot in any way remove the guilt or pardon the transgressor. He must go farther than this. The law is but the schoolmaster to bring him to Christ [see Galatians 3:24, 25]. He must look to his sin-bearing Saviour. And as Christ is revealed to him upon the cross of Calvary, dying beneath the weight of the sins of the whole world, the Holy Spirit shows him the attitude of God to all who repent of their transgressions. For God so loved the world, that He gave His only begotten Son, that whosoever believeth in Him should not perish, but have everlasting life (John 3:16).[3]

To fully understand this section of Scripture it must be read in context. The use made of it to support the idea that God was pleased with the people's pledge to obey is not sustained by the contextual reading of the entire section beginning with verse 24. The narrative reports that the people "said" many things such as: (1) a recognition that their God was real, unlike any of the gods they had known in Egypt; (2) how great,

----

3. Ellen G. White, *Selected Messages*, Book. 1, p. 213 (see also pp. 234-235; and *Ellen G. White 1888 Materials*, p. 1575).

powerful and magnificent God was; (3) that they were afraid of God as He had demonstrated Himself on Mount Sinai; (4) that no one could live in the presence of such a powerful Being; and (5) because of their fear, they wanted Moses to speak to them in God's behalf. However, only the very last clause of the verse immediately preceding is used by individuals who claim verse 28 is indicating that God approved of and accepted the people's promise to obey ("and we will hear it, and do it").

The *Jewish Publication Society Torah Commentary* on Deuteronomy has translated verses 27 and 28 thus:

> You go closer and hear all that the LORD our God says, and then you tell us everything that the LORD our God tells you, and we will willingly do it. The LORD heard the plea that you made to me [Moses], and the LORD said to me, "I have heard the plea that this people made to you; they did well to speak thus. May they be of such mind, to revere Me and follow all My commandments, that it may go well with them and with their children forever."

The commentary on these verses is this:

> verse 27: **we will willingly do it**—Literally, "we will hear [what you tell us] and do it." This is a key moment in the narrative: the people pledge to accept Moses' reports of what God commands and to perform whatever laws he transmits to them. They have voluntarily given up receiving the remaining laws from God personally, and they may not in the future disobey Moses or challenge what he reports to them.

> verse 28: God appreciates the reverence that leads the people to make their request. He hopes that this reverence will remain with them and motivate them to observe the commandments. Implicit in His words is the concern that as the experience recedes from the people's memory, so will their reverence.

From this commentary, it seems that what God is referring to when He said "they have well spoken" includes much more than simply the people's willingness to "obey" (last clause of verse 27). It includes at least these three things: His acceptance (1) of their reverence for Him as the Almighty Monarch of the universe, (2) of His recognition of their fear of Him, and (3) of their decision to let Moses be their intercessor between them and God.

We must remember that this decision to use Moses as their intercessor came after God spoke the second commandment (Exodus 20:1–4). It was at this point, after witnessing the "lightnings, and the noise of the trumpet, and the mountain smoking" that the people were so filled with fear of God that they ran away and said, "Moses, speak thou unto us, and we will hear: but let not God speak with us, lest we die" (Exodus 20:18, 19). The Hebrew grammar of the text in Exodus 20 indicates that after the second commandment, the pronouns switch from first to third person as God was now speaking through Moses rather than to the people directly. In writing Exodus chapter 20, Moses didn't break up the flow of the narrative to interject the people's objections which later appear in verses 18 and 19, but he did change the grammar to indicate their change in attitude and God's response to it.

The "implicit concern" that the *JPS Commentary* mentions would indicate that, while accepting what was valid of their words, God holds in reservation their promise to obey: "O, that there *were* such an heart in them, that they would fear Me, and keep all My commandments always. ..." Three times during the Sinai narrative, the people make the same promise to obey (Exodus 19:8; 24:3, 7). Significantly, all three times occur before the incident of the golden calf. After their sin with the golden calf, which violated the first two commandments, they learned what awaited them when they broke their vow of obedience. Though spoken in earnestness and with sincerity, through this experience they saw their utter inability to keep their promises. They also learned their God was a God of mercy, grace, longsuffering, and abundant in goodness and truth because He did not destroy the entire nation for their participation in this sin (which, based on their slave mentality, is what they deserved and expected).

In God's omniscience and foreknowledge He could see that their promise of obedience was to be short-lived and would end in the episode of the golden calf. Nonetheless (as He expressed in Deuteronomy 5:29), it was His sincere desire that the people would know Him, and love Him, and appreciate Him for who He truly was—their only Saviour, Provider, Protector and Friend. It was a lesson the nation as a whole never learned and which brought about their deportations to Assyria and Babylon. Finally, after their rejection of the Messiah and His crucifixion, it brought about their destruction and dispersion by the Roman armies in AD 70.

If the people *had* held such an heart-softening, respectful opinion of God, they would never have fallen into sin again, and their entire history from Sinai to Calvary would have been completely different. This was what God was attempting to teach them as they traveled through the desert to Sinai, but they never learned the lesson. Arriving at Sinai, they held the same opinion of God as when they left Egypt, even though they had seen numerous miracles and had been abundantly cared for by the Living Bread which came down from heaven, and by the Living Water gushing forth from the riven Rock.

A wrong view of God's character will always lead people to make mistakes in their theology. It caused the people of Jesus' day to have difficulty in making a distinction between the truth and the traditions and maxims of the Pharisees.[4] A wrong view of God's character is what keeps the world today in bondage to the sins of both legalism and antinomianism.

---

4. See *Desire of Ages*, p. 670.

8

Placed Under the Law

Elder E.J. Waggoner made a clear statement regarding the purpose of the law when he wrote:—

"But the Scripture hath concluded all under sin, that the promise by faith of Jesus Christ might be given to them that believe. But before faith came, we were kept under the law, shut up unto the faith which should afterwards be revealed. Wherefore the law was our schoolmaster to bring us unto Christ, that we might be justified by faith. But after that faith is come, we are no longer under a schoolmaster." Galatians 3:22–25. The law must be kept, and the terrors of Sinai were designed to drive them back to the oath of God [Genesis 15:17, 18; Hebrews 6:16–18], which four hundred and thirty years before had been given to stand to all people in all ages as the assurance of righteousness through the crucified and ever-living Saviour.[1]

Concurring fully with Waggoner's view on the covenant, A.T. Jones made the following comments regarding the promise of the people at Sinai:—

Why was the covenant at Sinai a covenant of bondage? Didn't they promise to obey and keep His law,—the Ten Commandments?—Certainly. And is not obedience to God in keeping of His law a good thing?—Unquestionably. Then wasn't it a good thing that they promised?—Most assuredly.

---

1. E.J. Waggoner, *The Glad Tidings* (Gordonsville, Tenn., CFI Book Division, 2016), p. 78.

Then what was the difficulty? Where was the fault?—The difficulty was not in the *thing* that they promised to do, but in their *promise* to do that thing. The covenant from Sinai is declared by the Scriptures to have been faulty: that it was faulty in the promises, and that the fault was found "with them." Hebrews 8:7, 8. Yet all that they did was to promise that they would obey the voice of God and keep the Ten Commandments. Therefore by the plain word of the Scriptures it was a fault for the people at Sinai to promise to obey God's voice and keep His law in order to have God be their God, and they to be His people. And this simply for the reason that they could not do it. It was therefore a fault for them to enter into a compact of "Obey and Live."

… Therefore, I now say deliberately and forever, that it is a fault for any person in the universe, either angel or man, at the beginning of his existence or at any other time, to promise to obey the law of God in order that he may have life or righteousness, or for any other purpose or for any reason whatever. It is a fault for either angels or men ever to enter into any compact of "Obey and Live," or to offer to God obedience as the satisfaction of a "condition" upon which "only" they can secure the promise of life. And this for the reason that under such a "compact" and upon such "condition" their obedience and therefore their righteousness would be only of themselves and of the law. And self-righteousness is no more true righteousness, and no more acceptable to God in a heavenly angel than it is in an earthly Pharisee.

… Righteousness, whether to men, to angels, to bright seraphim, or to exalted cherubim, comes not by obedience of their own, from their own "promise" under a "compact," upon "condition" and proviso. It comes only from the grace of God through the faith of Jesus Christ; never their own righteousness which is of the law, but always only "that which is through the faith of Christ, the righteousness which is of God by faith."

And in this word "faith" I mean not a mere theoretical notion, but "faith" in its only true meaning of the *will submitted* to Him, the *heart yielded* to Him, and the *affections fixed* upon Him. This only is faith; and this itself by the grace and gift of God. And this faith, of the will submitted to God *through*

Christ, of the heart yielded to God *in* Christ, and the affections fixed upon God *by* Christ—this is the faith of angels as truly as of men.[2]

2. A.T. Jones, *The Everlasting Gospel of the Everlasting Covenant*, (pp.16, 17, 19); is a self published document composed of remarks Jones made in the Battle Creek Sanitarium Sabbath School on July 20, 1907 (emphasis in original). In this document Jones addresses the persistent old covenantism present in the 1907 General Conference *Adult Sabbath School Quarterly*. In the last paragraph Jones defines faithful allegiance to God—"the *will submitted* ... the *heart yielded* ... the *affections fixed**." A PDF reproduction of this full document is available for study at: http://www.gospel-herald.com/pdf_files/jones_1907_ss_remarks.pdf

9

God's Original Objective Thwarted

God was forced to deal with the children of Israel in ways other than what He had planned when they insisted on remaining under the old covenant, vassal (or slave) mentality. At Sinai, God's original purpose was to meet with His people face to face for a marriage ceremony. The people were at first amenable to that event even though they did not understand it. In their pride they assumed they were ready to meet the unveiled and unmediated presence of their Lord. "Although God knows full well that Bnei Yisrael cannot possibly sustain a direct encounter with the '*Shchinah*' [sic], He nonetheless concedes to their request to hear the Commandments directly."[1]

God instructed Moses that the people were to spend three days in preparation for this divine appointment. He would then descend on the mountain in their view.

> All the defilements gathered by the way, all the dust of the conflict with Amalek had to be washed off; and short of water as they had lately been, God, we may be sure, provided an abundant supply before giving this command. He required his people through certain symbolic actions to enter into a special state of readiness for Himself. Then when they were so far ready by what they did to themselves, they must take further special precautions not to enter on the holy ground. As God took from the dwellers of the earth the house of Jacob to be his holy nation, so he took these steeps of Sinai to be a holy

---

1. Rabbi Menachem Leibtag, "Parshat Yitro—The Four Stages of Maamad Har Sinai." Document retrieved September 3, 2003 from http://www.tanach.org/shmot/yitro/yitros1.htm

place for himself. Evidently all these preparations being of the character they were, must have produced a state of mind full of expectation and suspense.[2]

On the third day, the people assembled at the foot of Mount Sinai at the specified safety distance. Only Moses and Aaron were allowed to enter the actual vicinity of the mountain (Exodus 19:20–25). The mountain began to rumble with the glory of the *Shechinah* as He spoke His commandments, and the people were afraid (vs. 16). In response to their fear, God commanded Moses to descend the mountain and assure the people of their safety (vs. 25).

According to a detailed linguistic analysis of the original Hebrew text, Exodus 20:18 should be read as actually occurring after God spoke the first two commandments. It was all the people could tolerate of God's magnificence before they cried out in fear, asking Moses to be the spokesman for God because they were afraid the presence of God would kill them. Moses transcribed the commandments without this interruption, but the original Hebrew indicates the grammar shifts from the first to the third person after the second commandment, indicating the first two commandments were spoken directly from God to the people, whereas the remaining commandments were related through Moses.[3]

Why did the people change their minds? Why did the sight of the glory of God frighten them? Was there ever a time when a human being faced the *Shechinah* glory without fear? Abraham was visited by the same *Shechinah* when God sealed the covenant with him (Genesis 15:17). A "smoking furnace and a burning lamp" passed before Abraham while he gazed in rapturous wonderment. Moses also faced the *Shechinah* in the burning bush. Out of reverence and cautious trepidation, Moses at first hid his face from the mysterious sight, but he didn't attempt to run and hide (Exodus 3:3–6). Prior to these events, Abraham and Moses both went through a reorientation program which deepened and focused their faith and dependence in and upon the one, true God.[4]

In contrast, we see the children of Israel trembling and running away from the theophany on the mountain. The fear experienced by the children of Israel was a result of their own unconverted heart and

---

2. *The Pulpit Commentary; Genesis and Exodus* (Grand Rapids, Michigan, Wm. B. Eerdmans, n.d.) volume 1.

3. Leibtag, Ibid.

4. See article "Moses," Ellen G. White, *Signs of the Times*, February 19, 1880, and *Patriarchs and Prophets*, pp. 147-153.

piteous lack of faith in God's love for them. Abraham and Moses stand in stark contrast to the unconverted condition of the children of Israel at Sinai.

Abraham and Moses had true faith in God and were unafraid to be in His holy presence, friend with friend. Because the children of Israel had failed to learn the lessons God attempted to teach them on their way through the wilderness, He allowed them to experience this frightening event at Sinai to reveal to them their essential need of conversion. This incident exhibits to us how much He desired to bring them to a true knowledge of their spiritual condition—wretched, miserable, poor, blind and naked, and in desperate need of everything God wanted to give them—if they only would have the faith of their father Abraham.

However, the children of Israel insisted on living like vassals instead of free children of the King of the universe. Despite all the blessings God had poured out upon them, He could not get them to change their inclination toward self-dependence, nor change their attitude of unbelief and grumbling. Now as He met with them at Sinai, ready to elevate them to the exalted position of His ambassadors to the lost world, He could do nothing else except meet them where they were in their slave mentality.

During their three month's journey to meet Him at His holy mountain, they had proven their hearts were stone, resistant to the molding He had attempted to do. God's original desire was to write His laws upon their soft, pliant hearts as He had done with their fathers Abraham, Isaac and Jacob.[5] However, since they persisted in functioning from their vassal perspective, He would write His laws on tablets of stone, reflecting their own condition of heart.

What followed was the giving of a suzerain contract matching what they, in their persistent unbelief, thought they had been living under all along. The people had unitedly spoken: "All that You say, we will do." Because of their sin of unbelief, the suzerain contract was made with them at Sinai to show them they could not do what they promised. Less than two months later, they were worshiping the golden calf and crying to return to Egypt.

While Moses was on the mountain, the people became restless. Though they failed to learn dependence upon God, they had learned dependence upon Moses and now he appeared to have deserted them in the desert. Facing Aaron they demanded that he craft them a god of

---

5. Genesis 26:5; Jeremiah 31:33; Hebrews 8:9-11.

gold; something tangible they could see and touch. This god would take the place of Moses; they would place their dependence upon a golden calf. Besides being a reversion to their Egyptian pantheistic notions and decadent behaviors, this act was a blatant violation of the first and second stipulations of the suzerain covenant they had arrogantly agreed to keep just a few weeks before.

When God instructed Moses to return to the camp, He told him: "Go, get thee down; for thy people, which thou broughtest out of the land of Egypt, have corrupted themselves: they have turned aside quickly out of the way which I commanded them: they have made them a molten calf, and have worshipped it, and have sacrificed thereunto, and said, These be thy gods, O Israel, which have brought thee up out of the land of Egypt. And the LORD said unto Moses, I have seen this people, and, behold, it is a stiffnecked people:[6] now therefore let Me alone, that My wrath may wax hot against them, and that I may consume them: and I will make of thee a great nation." (Exodus 32:7–10).

Our traditional interpretation of these verses has been that this was a test of Moses' character, which indeed it was. However, it was also an accurate judgment and condemnation on the part of the Suzerain against His covenant-violating vassals. God no longer claimed the people as His own special possession as was His expressed desire (Exodus 19:3–6). They were now Moses' problem, which reflected the people's attitude. Under the suzerain covenant, there was no mercy for the violator of the stipulations. God had justification for saying He was going to wipe this people from the face of the earth.

What changed? Why were the people spared from sudden destruction? Moses reminded God of His everlasting covenant which He revealed to Abraham, renewed with Isaac and then Jacob. "Remember Abraham, Isaac, and Israel, Thy servants, to whom Thou swarest by Thine own self, and saidst unto them, I will multiply your seed as the stars of heaven, and all this land that I have spoken of will I give unto your seed, and they shall inherit it for ever" (Exodus 32:13). God is a covenant-keeping God; His everlasting covenant can never be broken because it stands

---

6. For nearly fifteen centuries God called Israel "stiffnecked" for their persistent refusal to believe in the promise of God for salvation from sin, "Ye stiffnecked and uncircumcised in heart and ears, ye do always resist the Holy Ghost: as your fathers did, so do ye. Which of the prophets have not your fathers persecuted? and they have slain them which shewed before of the coming of the Just One; of whom ye have been now the betrayers and murderers: Who have received the law by the disposition of angels, and have not kept it." (Acts 7:51-53).

on the "better promises" of God Himself to save from sin (Hebrews 8:6; Matthew 1:21). And so He "repented" (Exodus 32:14).

Moses was concerned about God's holy name, about His character, and about what the surrounding nations would say about Him if He destroyed the people He had delivered from Egyptian bondage. "Wherefore should the Egyptians speak, and say, for mischief did He bring them out, to slay them in the mountains, and to consume them from the face of the earth?"

Moses had no knowledge of what had been taking place below him on the plain around Mount Sinai in his absence. He could now wonder at God's change in attitude toward His people. "Why doth Thy wrath wax hot against Thy people, which Thou hast brought forth out of the land of Egypt with great power, and with a mighty hand?"

When Moses descended the mountain with Joshua, he soon understood God's anger. In his disgust at the people's abject disloyalty to their one true God, Moses smashed the tables which contained the stipulations of the covenant written by the finger of God (Exodus 31:18), a symbolic action signifying the broken covenant. One could analogize by saying that the "ink" wasn't even dry on the contract before the people had broken every promise they had made to their Suzerain.

> At Sinai the people promised to keep the given law. But in their own strength they had no power to keep the law. Mount Sinai "bore children for slavery," since their promise to make themselves righteous by their own works was not successful and can never be …
>
> Then did not God Himself lead them into bondage? Not by any means, since He did not induce them to make that covenant at Sinai. Four hundred and thirty years before that time He had made a covenant with Abraham which was sufficient for all purposes. That covenant was confirmed in Christ, and therefore was a covenant from above. See John 8:23. It promised righteousness as a free gift of God through faith, and it included all nations. All the miracles that God had wrought in delivering the children of Israel from Egyptian bondage were but demonstrations of His power to deliver them (and us) from the bondage of sin. Yes, the deliverance from Egypt was itself a demonstration not only of God's power but also of His desire to lead them from the bondage of sin.

So, when the people came to Sinai, God simply referred them to what He had already done and then said: "Now therefore, if ye will obey My voice indeed, and keep My covenant, then ye shall be a peculiar treasure unto Me above all people: for all the earth is Mine. Exodus 19:5. To what covenant did He refer? Evidently to the one already in existence, His covenant with Abraham. If they would simply keep God's covenant, keep the faith, and believe God's promise, they would be a "peculiar treasure" unto God. As the possessor of all the earth, He was able to do for them all that He had promised.

The fact that they in their self-sufficiency rashly took the whole responsibility upon themselves does not prove that God had led them to make that covenant.[7]

Leaving Sinai, never-ending rebellion remained the norm for the children of Israel as they marched onward to the border of the Promised Land. After the golden calf incident, we read about their pining for Egypt and its food; Miriam and Aaron's insurrection; the evil report of the spies and the resulting forty years of wandering; the rebellion of Korah, Dathan, and Abiram; and repeated bellyaching which sprang from their persistent unbelief and resulting discouragement. Through it all, God was giving and forgiving, but the people failed to comprehend either their true helpless, sinful condition or God's mercy and love.[8] The covenant made at Sinai could only perpetuate a vassal mentality and its consequent bondage.

---

7. E.J. Waggoner, *The Glad Tidings*, pp. 98-99; emphasis in original.

8. The sin of refusing to know is also recognized as the primary sin of Laodicea, God's remnant church (Revelation 3:17).

10

Suzerain Covenant
Restated to Israel

Forty years passed. Moses stood before the people at Kadesh-Barnea, reminding the children of their dead fathers' sins. "The LORD made this covenant with us at Horeb. The LORD made not this covenant with our fathers, but with us, even us, who are all of us here alive this day" (Deuteronomy 5:2, 3). Moses was speaking corporately to the second generation, but was including the previous generation who all died in the wilderness because of their unbelief and rebellion at Kadesh-Barnea (Numbers 13:31–33). Here Moses plainly declared that the covenant made with the people at Sinai was not the same one God made with "our fathers"— Abraham, Isaac, and Jacob.

The original, everlasting covenant was a promise founded on the solid Rock, which is Christ (Deuteronomy 32:4–31; 1 Corinthians 10:4). It is a covenant of faith based on believing that God is powerful enough to accomplish His promise. The promise included making righteous all who would believe, recreating us into a holy nation of kings and priests, who will vindicate the character of God. "But ye are a chosen generation, a royal priesthood, an holy nation, a peculiar people; that ye should shew forth the praises of Him who hath called you out of darkness into His marvellous light" (1 Peter 2:9; see also Revelation 1:5, 6; 5:10; 14:12).

The covenant made with the children's fathers at Sinai rested only on the unstable sands of human pledges. Careful reading of verses 2 through 4 reveals the corporate idea that the people assembled at Kadesh-Barnea were viewed as being the same ones who were standing at Sinai forty years before who promised God they would fulfill the covenant stipulations. As previously discussed, Moses said the covenant made with them at that time (forty years before) was not the same covenant God made with their fathers, Abraham, Isaac and Jacob.

Scripture relates that it is the promise made to Abraham, Isaac, and Jacob which constitutes the reality of the everlasting covenant. Through their continued rebellion the people had proven themselves to be unworthy of any blessing, but God is faithful to His promise to the fathers, Abraham, Isaac and Jacob. This promise is the basis for the children of Israel's possession of the land of Canaan. Moses made this clear whenever he discussed Israel's history. Later in his address to the children of the rebels at Kadesh-Barnea, Moses said:—

> Not for thy righteousness, or for the uprightness of thine heart, dost thou go to possess their land: but for the wickedness of these nations the LORD thy God doth drive them out from before thee, and that He may perform the word which the LORD sware unto thy fathers, Abraham, Isaac, and Jacob. Understand therefore, that the LORD thy God giveth thee not this good land to possess it for thy righteousness; for thou art a stiffnecked people (Deuteronomy 9:5, 6).

As Moses concluded this section of his address, he turned his attention from a rehearsal of their sordid history to a prayer in their behalf. Again, he recalled the promise to Abraham, Isaac and Jacob. Speaking to God in behalf of the people he said: "Remember Thy servants, Abraham, Isaac, and Jacob; look not unto the stubbornness of this people, nor to their wickedness nor to their sin" (9:27). Why?—because Moses was concerned for God's character; he was worried about what the people of the surrounding nations would say about God if He didn't deliver on His promise to Abraham, Isaac, and Jacob (verses 28 and 29).

After Moses finished his farewell speech to the people he had shepherded for forty years, he was gently laid in his grave. The staff of leadership having passed to Joshua, the people march to the Jordan River, where under the command of Christ, the Captain of God's army, the children of Israel had no difficulty in conquering Jericho (Joshua 5:13–15; chapter 6).

However, by the time they approached Ai, pride had begun its work in their hearts. Their success at Jericho was viewed as being a result of their own power, not God's. Therefore, following their own plans, they thought they could conquer Ai without consultation from the Captain of the Lord's army (7:3–5). Additionally, the explicit command that everything in Jericho was dedicated to God (6:17–19) was scorned, which brought condemnation to the whole camp of Israel. Both of these factors brought defeat at Ai. Both reveal a lack of respect for and genuine knowledge about who God is. After cleansing the camp of its sin, Ai was taken through ambush. Following this victory, Joshua built an altar to God and read the Sinai covenant before all the people (8:30–35).

Joshua's reading of the covenant before the people follows the suzerain contract formula for contract renewal, as discussed previously in chapter two. It was the means for familiarizing the entire populace with their obligations to God, the great King of Israel. We find a few more instances in the Old Testament where the Sinai covenant was read before the people in a renewal ceremony. Josiah's reformation is one example (2 Kings 23:1–3).

All these efforts at reformation were short-lived. The people soon forgot their obligations and returned to their self-centered interests and self-dependence. The covenant at Sinai was never strong enough to motivate the people to faithfully serve God. Neither is it today. Many people, even today, say they believe in God when in fact their motivation is a fear of hell and misunderstanding of God's character of love. The depth of His love and completeness of His everlasting covenant (Romans 8:37–39), was never comprehended by the majority of the people.

11

New Testament Commentary on the Sinaitic Events

The apostle Paul tells us that the covenant made at Sinai was condemnable, full of fault, being founded on the faulty promises of the people. It could only keep the people bound in slavery. That this was not God's intention is made plain in Paul's letter to the Hebrews. Quoting Jeremiah, Paul writes:—

For if that first *covenant*[1] had been faultless, then should no place have been sought for the second. For finding fault with them [the children of Israel], He saith, Behold, the days come, saith the LORD, when I will make a new covenant with the house of Israel[2] and with the house of Judah: not according to the covenant that I made with their fathers in the day when I took them by the hand to lead them out of the land of Egypt; because they continued not in My covenant, and I regarded them not, saith the LORD.

For this is the covenant that I will make with the house of Israel after those days, saith the LORD; I will put My laws into their mind, and write them in their hearts: and I will be to them a God, and they shall be to Me a people: and they shall not teach every man his neighbour, and every man his brother, saying, Know the LORD: for all shall know Me, from the least to the greatest. For I will be merciful to their unrighteousness, and their sins and their iniquities will I remember no more. In

---

1. The word "covenant" is supplied by the translators and is not found in the original text. Paul is here refering to the priesthood discussion in chapter 7.
2. "The house of Israel" (or "family") in the Biblical sense consists of all people who by faith become heirs of the promise given to Abraham. Romans 4:13-16; 9:6-8; Galatians 3:18, 28, 29.

that He saith, A new *covenant*, He hath made the first old. Now that which decayeth and waxeth old is ready to vanish away (Hebrews 8:7–13; cf. Jeremiah 31:31–34).

From these verses it is clear that God never intended to write His laws on tablets of stone at Sinai. He intended to write the laws on His people's converted hearts, just like He had with Abraham and Isaac and Jacob. However, the people's persistent unbelief prevented that from taking place. The nation of Israel chose to live under the old covenant, living as a vassal to the mighty Suzerain while rejecting the spiritual rest God had planned for them as His adopted children. Paul appeals to the Jews of his day not to repeat this sin of unbelief. The appeal remains for us today, if we will hear His voice.[3]

The exhortation of the apostle applies to us as well as to those to whom this epistle was directed. "Let us therefore fear, lest, a promise being left us of entering into His rest, any of you should seem to come short of it. For unto us was the gospel preached, as well as unto them." Christ taught the people the principles of Christianity, speaking from the pillar of cloud and of fire, by day and by night; but they did not obey His words, and the apostle presents before us the consequence of their disobedience, stating that they were overthrown in the wilderness because of their rebellion. He says, "For unto us was the gospel preached, as well as unto them; but the word preached did not profit them, not being mixed with faith in them that heard it." Shall we who are living near the close of this world's history "take heed"? Shall we heed the apostle's warning, "Let us therefore fear, lest, a promise being left us of entering into His rest, any of you should seem to come short of it"?[4]

Wherefore (as the Holy Ghost saith, To day if ye will hear His voice, harden not your hearts, as in the provocation, in the day of temptation in the wilderness: when your fathers tempted Me, proved Me, and saw My works forty years. Wherefore I was grieved with that generation, and said, They do alway err in their heart; and they have not known My ways. So I sware in My wrath, They shall not enter into My rest.) Take heed,

---

3. Ellen G. White, "Danger in Rejecting Light," *Review and Herald*, October 21, 1890.
4. Ibid.

brethren, lest there be in any of you an evil heart of unbelief, in departing from the living God. But exhort one another daily, while it is called To day; lest any of you be hardened through the deceitfulness of sin. For we are made partakers of Christ, if we hold the beginning of our confidence stedfast unto the end; while it is said, To day if ye will hear His voice, harden not your hearts, as in the provocation.

For some, when they had heard, did provoke: howbeit not all that came out of Egypt by Moses. But with whom was He grieved forty years? was it not with them that had sinned, whose carcases fell in the wilderness? And to whom sware He that they should not enter into His rest, but to them that believed not? So we see that they could not enter in because of unbelief (Hebrews 3:7–19).

Why was the law given in the written, hard copy form at Sinai? Paul tells us the law was a schoolmaster to bring the people to Christ (Galatians 3:24). Because of the hardness of their hearts, it was required to write the law on tablets of stone as a visible reminder of what they couldn't see by faith, and to convict them of their utter inability, in their own strength, to live up to God's standard.

But there was a still greater truth to be impressed upon their minds. Living in the midst of idolatry and corruption, they had no true conception of the holiness of God, of the exceeding sinfulness of their own hearts, their utter inability, in themselves, to render obedience to God's law, and their need of a Saviour. All this they must be taught. ... The people did not realize the sinfulness of their own hearts, and that without Christ it was impossible for them to keep God's law; and they readily entered into covenant with God. Feeling that *they were able to establish their own righteousness*, they declared, All that the Lord hath said will we do, and be obedient. Exodus 24:7. They had witnessed the proclamation of the law in awful majesty, and had trembled with terror before the mount; and yet only a few weeks passed before they broke their covenant with God, and bowed down to worship a graven image. They could not hope for the favor of God through a covenant which they had broken; and now, seeing their sinfulness and their need of pardon, they were brought to feel their need of the Saviour revealed in the Abrahamic covenant and shadowed forth in the sacrificial offerings.[5]

It is by the law of God that the sinner is convicted. He sees his own sinfulness in contrast with the perfect righteousness which it enjoins, and this leads him to humility and repentance. He becomes reconciled to God through the blood of Christ, and as he continues to walk with Him he will be gaining a clearer sense of the holiness of God's character and the far-reaching nature of His requirements. He will see more clearly his own defects and will feel the need of continual repentance and faith in the blood of Christ.[6]

This was God's intention when giving the children of Israel the law at Sinai, however, they persisted in sinful unbelief thwarting the purposes of their Suzerain Lord. Determined minds and reliance on self, the essence of a contractual agreement, kept the people bound under faithless obligation to an external code of ethics. They remained "under law."

"But before faith came, we were kept under the law, shut up unto the faith which should afterwards be revealed. Wherefore the law was our schoolmaster to bring us unto Christ, that we might be justified by faith." (Galatians 3:23-24).

Before faith came we were confined under the law, "shut up" unto the faith which should afterwards be revealed. We know that whatsoever is not of faith is sin (Romans 14:23); therefore, to be "under the law" is identical with being under sin. The grace of God brings salvation from sin so that when we believe God's grace we are no longer under the law, because we are freed from sin. Those who are under the law therefore are the transgressors of the law. The righteous are not under it, but are walking in it.

The Revised Standard Version renders "custodian" in the place of the King James Version's "schoolmaster." The German

5. White, "The Law and the Covenants," *Patriarchs and Prophets*, p. 371-372 (emphasis supplied): Note that she contrasts the covenant made at Sinai with the covenant made with Abraham, making a clear distinction between the these two covenants. She further emphasizes that the one made with Abraham was the one the people needed for their salvation because it is based on a faith-response to God's promise.

6. White, *Faith and Works*, (Nashville, Tenn.: Southern Publishing, 1979), pp. 53-54.

and Scandinavian translations employ a word which signifies "master of a house of correction."

The Greek word comes down to us in English as "pedagogue." The *paidagogos* was the father's slave who accompanied the father's boys to school to see that they did not play truant. If they attempted to run away he would bring them back and had authority even to beat them to keep them in the way. The word has come to be used as meaning "schoolmaster," although the Greek word does not convey the idea of a schoolmaster. "Supervisor or "custodian" would be better. The one under this custodian, although nominally at large, is really deprived of his liberty just the same as though he were actually in a cell. The fact is that all who do not believe are under sin," "shut up" "under the law," and, therefore, the law acts as their supervisor or custodian. It is the law that will not let them go. The guilty cannot escape in their guilt. Although God is merciful and gracious, He will not clear the guilty. Exodus 34:6, 7. That is, He will not lie by calling evil good. But He provides a way by which the guilty may lose their guilt. Then the law will no longer curtail their liberty and they can walk free in Christ.[7]

However, in it's hard copy format, manifested under the old covenant suzerain contract formula, the covenant from Sinai could not countermand the original covenant God made with Abraham four hundred and thirty years before.

And this I say, that the covenant, that was confirmed before of God in Christ, the law, which was four hundred and thirty years after, cannot disannul, that it should make the promise of none effect. For if the inheritance be of the law, it is no more of promise: but God gave it to Abraham by promise. Wherefore then serveth the law? It was added because of transgressions, till the Seed should come to whom the promise was made; and

---

7. Waggoner, *The Glad Tidings*, pp. 80-81; emphasis in original. "The word conclude means literally confine, just as it is given in verse 23. Of course, a person who is confined by the law is in prison. In human governments a criminal is confined as soon as the law can get hold of him. God's law is everywhere present and always active. Therefore the instant a man sins he is confined. This is the condition of all the world, for all have sinned, and there is none righteous, no, not one." p. 79. The Gospel of Jesus and His righteousness was given to set the captives free from bondage to sin.

it was ordained by angels in the hand of a mediator (Galatians 3:17–19).

In a later section of this discussion we will examine in further detail the covenant significance of the inheritance promised to Abraham.

Paul continues with his comparison of the old and new covenants in Galatians chapter 4. Here he states that Abraham lived under the old covenant idea when he took Hagar to be his wife, hoping to produce the son of promise through her; attempting by his own works of the flesh to gain the reality of God's promise. However, Paul doesn't stop with the mistakes of Abraham. He brings the issue right down to the blunder made at Sinai, calling that the old covenant "which gendereth to bondage," which can never bring freedom to the ones who live under it.

> For it is written, that Abraham had two sons, the one by a bondmaid, the other by a freewoman. But he who was of the bondwoman was born after the flesh; but he of the freewoman was by promise. Which things are an allegory: for these are the two covenants; the one from the mount Sinai, which gendereth to bondage, which is Agar. For this Agar is mount Sinai in Arabia, and answereth to Jerusalem which now is, and is in bondage with her children. But Jerusalem which is above is free, which is the mother of us all (Galatians 4:22–26).

And again, in Hebrews 12:18–24, Paul makes a clear distinction between the covenant made with the children of Israel at Sinai and the everlasting covenant made with Abraham. After his discourse relating the long list of individuals who had lived by faith in the promise of God, those who looked for "that better country, that is, an heavenly," he concludes that section of his letter by admonishing us to heed the witnesses who have gone on before us. As these did, we also are to look "unto Jesus, the author and finisher of our faith" for the perfection of our characters.

Paul says that we are not called to come up to the mount that "burned with fire," but we are to "come to mount Sion, and unto the city of the living God, the heavenly Jerusalem, and to an innumerable company of angels, to the general assembly and church of the firstborn, which are written in heaven, and to God the Judge of all, and to the spirits of just men made perfect, and to Jesus the mediator of the new covenant, and to the blood of sprinkling, that speaketh better things than that of Abel." Sinai is here again associated with the covenant that "passed away," not the new or everlasting covenant. Zion, the New Jerusalem, is emblematic of the everlasting covenant.

From this brief examination, we can see that it was a heart problem with ancient Israel, and it remains a heart problem with us today.

> The apostle when speaking of Hagar and Sarah says: "These women are two covenants." These two covenants exist today. The two covenants are not matters of time, but of condition. Let no one flatter himself that he cannot be bound under the old covenant, thinking that its time has passed. The time for that is passed only in the sense that "the time past of our life may suffice us to have wrought the will of the Gentiles, when we walked in lasciviousness, lust, excess of wine, revelings, banquetings, and abominable idolatries." 1 Peter 4:3, KJV.[8]

God longed to give His people the spiritual rest they needed, but their unbelief prevented Him from doing all that He would. Their hearts remained unimpressible. "Today" persistent unbelief in God's promises to save us continues to prevent us from entering into God's eternal rest.

---

8. Waggoner, p. 100

12

Persistence of the Suzerain Mind-set Throughout Ancient Israel's History

When the children of the rebellion approached the border of the Promised Land for the second time, Moses rehearsed their history to them. Beginning with the promise made to the "fathers," Abraham, Isaac, and Jacob, Moses briefly outlined the rebellion that occurred 40 years before at Kadesh-Barnea.

> The LORD our God spake unto us in Horeb, saying, Ye have dwelt long enough in this mount: turn you, and take your journey, and go to the mount of the Amorites, and unto all the places nigh thereunto, in the plain, in the hills, and in the vale, and in the south, and by the sea side, to the land of the Canaanites, and unto Lebanon, unto the great river, the river Euphrates. Behold, I have set the land before you: go in and possess the land which the LORD sware unto your fathers, Abraham, Isaac, and Jacob, to give unto them and to their seed after them (Deuteronomy 1:6–8).

Continuing his narrative Moses related how at Kadesh-Barnea, unbelief was again the response to God's promise. First the unbelief was manifested in the desire to scout out the territory, to determine if they possessed the manpower to capture the land already possessed by a fierce people. "The request that spies be sent into Canaan showed a lack of faith; for God had told the people plainly that they were to take possession of the land. Why then did they need spies to search it? Had they put their trust in God, they could have gone straight in. God would have gone before them." [1]

---

1. Ellen G. White, *General Conference Bulletin*, March 30, 1903.

The spies returned with a mixed report. All declared that the land was wonderful, filled with a bounty of everything they could possibly want, crops ready for harvesting and houses already built and furnished. However, most of the spies brought a discouraging report of giants, high-walled cities, and ferocious warriors. Unbelief caused their parents to reject the promise of God in favor of a return trip to Egypt (Numbers 14:1–4). Forty years later, God still had to deal with the same unbelief as He attempted to bring the children of the rebellion into the land promised to Abraham, Isaac, and Jacob.

A pattern of unbelief is evident throughout the books of Joshua and Judges, finally ending with the declaration that "every man did that which was right in his own eyes." The books of Samuel open with an apostate priesthood and continued war with the Philistines. The Israelites had become as superstitious as their pagan neighbors, placing more confidence in the gold encrusted box than they had in the God of heaven. Repeatedly, this falsely placed confidence brought them defeat and disgrace. Throughout this period of prevailing unbelief one man arose to lead the people, continually calling them to "return unto the LORD with all your hearts, and put away the strange gods and Ashtaroth from among you and prepare your hearts unto the LORD and serve Him only, and He will deliver you from the hand of the Philistines." (1 Samuel 7:3).

By the time of Samuel three hundred years had passed since they came into possession of the Promised Land, but the people's attitude of unbelief remained unchanged. If they had only believed in the power of God's promise and the covenant He had made with their fathers Abraham, Isaac and Jacob, He would have delivered the entire land into their hands without a fight.[2] However, they insisted on doing things the hard way.

Repeatedly, Moses warned them that after they possessed the land they were to avoid all forms of false religion (see Deuteronomy 4:15–19; 5:6–9; 17:2–5, etc.). Bound in their unbelief, they were easy prey for the enemy of their souls and soon fell into idol worship, thus preventing God from working marvelously in their behalf. When finally for a time, they heeded the admonitions of the prophet Samuel and repented of their apostasy, the Lord delivered them from their enemies. "And the

---

2. Exodus 23:27-33. It is noted in this section of Scripture that the Israelites were admonished to never make a covenant with any of the surrounding nations, that doing so would cause them to follow their idolatrous practices. Because they would not heed the Lord's instruction, they did just what they were instructed not to do which eventually brought them into captivity.

cities which the Philistines had taken from Israel were restored to Israel, from Ekron even unto Gath; and the coasts thereof did Israel deliver out of the hands of the Philistines. And there was peace between Israel and the Amorites." (1 Samuel 7:4, 14).

Shortly thereafter, the people lost their perspective again. Focused on men instead of God, they rejected the theocracy ordained by their Sovereign Lord and clamored for an earthly king who could lead them into battle, a demand which set up the next five hundred years of misery. Under the reign of kings, some of the worst apostasy and greatest evils took place in the nation of Israel, finally ending with their captivity in Babylon. As their own government and power were crumbling, this era was marked by political intrigue and numerous covenants with the surrounding nations as one Israelite king after another sought peace through alliance with the pagan kings around them. However, having turned their back on their true Sovereign, it was fruitless for them to seek peace through compromise with paganism.

To-day the Christian world looks upon the Jews as a people who are under the divine curse because of their rejection and crucifixion of Christ. But, instead of looking upon them as sinners above all others, they should seek to learn a lesson from their condition, and inquire why it is that the judgment of God fell upon them in so signal a manner. It was because they rejected the great light which had been given them from the time of their delivery from Egyptian bondage. It was because the Lord had revealed to them, through his prophets, and through holy men of old, His will, and they chose to walk in their own ways, and to follow their own will. Calamity overtook the Jews because they failed to keep the commandments of God. God had told them if they did not keep His commandments, He could not fulfill His *covenant of promise*, for this covenant was to be fulfilled only upon condition of obedience. The history of Israel should be to us a most solemn warning of the calamities that will overtake us if we are disobedient to God's commandments.[3]

---

3. White, "Obedience to God's Word Required," *Signs of the Times*, January 24, 1895.

Part III

Israel's Breach of the Covenant Contract

13

Covenants of Israel with Assyria

In the following sections we will examine a condensed assessment of the political history of Israel as it pertains to the suzerain covenant. Throughout the time of the divided kingdom, we find various suzerain contracts being made with surrounding nations. Along with the religious apostasy, these were a direct violation of the stipulations of the suzerain covenant made with God at Sinai, opening the way for a covenant lawsuit against them. It was a period of great political instability, treachery, and war. David's reign is purposely skipped; it will be discussed in a later section of this study.

During the tumultuous years after the kingdom was divided into Israel on the north and Judah on the south, we read of various covenants and treaties being made between Israelite kings and the sovereigns of the surrounding nations, and between Israel and God in which the people were the initiators. Many of these self-initiated treaties were hastily made and short-lived.

In 2 Kings 15:13–20 we read of a usurper to the throne of Israel who, in a political alliance, paid heavy tribute to Pul (Tiglath-pileser III) the king of Assyria. Menahem paid this tribute for the express purpose of maintaining his uncertain position as the ruler of Israel. However, by this time Assyria had ventured deeply into Palestine, and the Philistines were pushing from the west. Tiglath-pileser used wholesale transplantations of his conquered foes as a means of destroying nationalistic spirit and political sentiments. Many Israelites were being relocated out of Israel as Assyria over-ran the area (2 Kings 17:20–27). It was a highly unstable political era.

When Pekah, a usurper to the throne of Israel, challenged Ahaz, king of Judah, Ahaz set about to buy assistance from Tiglath-pileser by sending him the sacred vessels from the Temple of God (2 Kings 16:7–9). Through this act Ahaz insulted the Lord and proved to the world that he thought an earthly king had more power than the King of the universe. As a result, "the LORD brought Judah low because of Ahaz king of Israel; for he made Judah naked, and transgressed sore against the LORD." (2 Chronicles 28:19). Tiglath-pileser responded by invading Israel and Damascus and capturing much of that territory. While Tiglath-pileser was still at Damascus, Ahaz went to meet him and paid him tribute as his vassal (2 Kings 16:10).

Back in the northern kingdom, Hoshea assassinated Pekah and captured Israel's throne while Tiglath-pileser was campaigning in southwestern Palestine against the Philistines. Shortly thereafter, Tiglath-pileser was succeeded by Shalmaneser V. When Shalmaneser arrived in Palestine, Hoshea paid his suzerain tribute and was confirmed in the kingship (2 Kings 17:3). Hoshea paid tribute to Assyria for several years, then formed an alliance with Egypt in an effort to be free from Assyrian domination. After three years of constant siege against Samaria (the northern capital), Shalmaneser captured Hoshea and took him to Assyria where he died. There was never another king in the northern division. Their continual violation of the suzerain covenant made with God at Sinai brought the curses upon them and destruction of their nation.[1]

Hosea poignantly portrays this through his marriage to Gomer as recorded in his book. The final judgment of Israel is consequent upon the sin of Jehu in making a suzerain covenant with Assyria, which was the ultimate insult to the true Suzerain of Israel.

> The sin of Jehu turns out to be Israel's entry through Jehu into an alliance with Assyria, to which in its enduring form Hosea, more than a century later, is implacably opposed. The birth of a second child, "Not pitied," spells the end of the northern kingdom; the future hope lies with Judah (vv. 6, 7). However, the birth of the third child, "Not my people," spells the end of the covenant with Israel as a whole (1:8, 9). The name is the ultimate word of judgment, the ultimate breach of the marriage relationship.[2]

---

1. Deuteronomy 28:58-67; 30:15-20. Even in the curse against their disobedience, God calls to mind His promise to Abraham, Isaac, and Jacob as the source of His mercy and longsuffering with His rebellious nation. This divine promise is the source of all blessings; rejection of this promise is the source of all curses, and ultimately, destruction.
2. William J. Dumbrell, *The Faith of Israel* (Grand Rapids, Mich.: Baker Academic, 2002), p. 172.

Because of the promise He made with their fathers Abraham, Isaac, and Jacob, the Lord had been longsuffering with His rebellious vassal. "And the LORD was gracious unto them, and had compassion on them, and had respect unto them, because of his covenant with Abraham, Isaac, and Jacob, and would not destroy them, neither cast he them from his presence as yet." (2 Kings 13:23).

Later, Jeremiah declared that God's very name is a pledge of His fidelity to His promise. God not only makes the promise but is more than able to establish and carry out His promise to mankind (the everlasting covenant). The "great and mighty things" that He desired to show His people was salvation from their sins, salvation from their dependence upon themselves, and the power of life everlasting through faith in His promise (see Jeremiah 33:2, 3).[3]

This was a lesson the people never seemed to learn. Because of their stubborn iniquity, eventually divine forbearance was exhausted, "and the king of Assyria did carry away Israel unto Assyria, and put them in Halah and in Habor by the river of Gozan, and in the cities of the Medes: because they obeyed not the voice of the LORD their God, but transgressed His covenant, and all that Moses the servant of the LORD commanded, and would not hear them, nor do them." (2 Kings 18:11, 12).

---

3. H.D.M. Spence and Joseph S. Exell, eds., *The Pulpit Commentary; Jeremiah and Lamentations* (Grand Rapids, Mich.: Eerdmans, 1962), vol. II, p. 68.

14

Contracts of Judah with Assyria and Chaldea

While lingering for nearly 150 years after Assyria destroyed the northern division, as the northern tribes had done before them Judah repeatedly broke the covenant they made with God at Sinai by forming alliances with the nations around them. This would bring them down to captivity in Babylon. Ahaz's son Hezekiah attempted to overturn his father's deplorable subservience to Assyria. Through faith in God's power and ability to protect the nation, Hezekiah regained control over the Philistine lowlands (2 Kings 18:8), restored the sheepfolds and storage towns (2 Chronicles 32:27–29), fortified the wall around Jerusalem (Isaiah 22:10), and built the pool of Siloam to provide water to Jerusalem during war-time siege (2 Kings 20:20). However, for all his good deeds, Hezekiah refused to listen to the word of the Lord through Isaiah (Isaiah 30:1–5; 31:1–3), forming an alliance with Egypt and Ethiopia. This resulted in a speedy retaliation from Sennacherib who had succeeded to the throne of Assyria in 705 BC.

When Hezekiah witnessed what Assyria did to his brethren in the northern division of the nation, he repented. However, he committed the same sin Ahaz had committed. He foolishly sent Sennacherib silver and gold from the house of the Lord (2 Kings 18:13–16). Sennacherib ascertained this to be a weakness in Hezekiah that he could exploit.[1]

---

1. The inscriptions on a clay hexagonal prism tell of the conquests of Sennacherib. A section is translated as follows: "Hezekiah the Judaean [is] like a caged bird within the city of Jerusalem his capital city I shut up." Norman L. Geisler, *A Popular Survey of the Old Testament* (Grand Rapids, Mich.: Baker Books, 2003), p. 142. Interestingly, the glyphs translated "I shut up" literally spell "šú e - sír - šú" or *suzerain*. The ancient suzerain "shut up" his vassals with the stipulations of the contract.

While Sennacherib was occupied at Lachish, he sent emissaries to Hezekiah in an effort to persuade him to return fully to his allegiance and avoid outright war (2 Kings 19:17–35). This time Hezekiah appealed for assistance to the King of heaven, the original Suzerain of Israel, and in one night the angel of the Lord killed 185,000 Assyrians as they encamped around Jerusalem (v. 35).

Hezekiah's son was more evil than any of his predecessors. "Moreover Manasseh shed innocent blood very much, till he had filled Jerusalem from one end to another; beside his sin wherewith he made Judah to sin, in doing that which was evil in the sight of the LORD." (2 Kings 21:16). As a result of his wickedness, judgment was promised against Jerusalem and Judah.

> Because Manasseh king of Judah hath done these abominations, and hath done wickedly above all that the Amorites did, which were before him, and hath made Judah also to sin with his idols: therefore thus saith the LORD God of Israel, Behold, I am bringing such evil upon Jerusalem and Judah, that whosoever heareth of it, both his ears shall tingle. And I will stretch over Jerusalem the line of Samaria, and the plummet of the house of Ahab: and I will wipe Jerusalem as a man wipeth a dish, wiping it, and turning it upside down. And I will forsake the remnant of Mine inheritance, and deliver them into the hand of their enemies; and they shall become a prey and a spoil to all their enemies; because they have done that which was evil in My sight, and have provoked Me to anger, since the day their fathers came forth out of Egypt, even unto this day (vv. 11–15).

Manasseh apparently felt compelled to pay homage to his overlord's gods and filled Judah with idolatrous worship practices, including wizardry, Baal worship, and human sacrifice to Molech. His rampant persecution of God's faithful witnesses and prophets led Josephus to report of daily executions.[2] Much like Israel in the days of Ahab and Elijah, confusion reigned regarding who the true God really was. Apostasy crept in through slow increments and neglect of truth.

> It is, to be sure, probable that much of this represented no conscious abandonment of the national religion. The nature of

---

2. Flavius Josephus, *Antiquities of the Jews*, X iii 2, reproduced in *The Complete Works of Josephus*, (Grand Rapids. Mich.: Kregel, 1981), p. 214.

primitive Yahwism had been so widely forgotten, and the rites incompatible with it so long practiced, that in many minds the essential distinction between Yahweh and the pagan gods had been obscured. It was possible for such people to practice these rites alongside the cult of Yahweh without awareness that they were turning from the national faith in doing so. The situation was one of immense, and in some ways novel, danger to the religious integrity of Israel. Yahwism was in danger of slipping unawares into outright polytheism … the decay of the national religion brought with it contempt of Yahweh's laws and new incidents of violence and injustice (Zeph. 1:9; 3:1–7), together with a skepticism regarding Yahweh's ability to act in events (ch. 1:12). Hezekiah's reform was canceled completely and the voice of prophecy silenced; those who protested—and apparently there were those who did—were dealt with severely (2 Kings 21:16).[3]

Under Manasseh's rule, the foreign powers of Moab and Ammon began to revolt. To settle the political unrest in the area, the Assyrians bound Manasseh in chains and transported him to Babylon (2 Chronicles 33:11). While imprisoned in Babylon and hating the miserableness of his predicament, Manasseh had a change of heart. The God of his fathers heard his supplications and restored him to the throne in Judah.

However, after his death Manasseh's reformation was rapidly undone by his wicked son, Amon, who was so vile that even his own people detested him. They murdered him after a two year reign and placed his eight year old son, Josiah, on the throne. While accomplishing his religious reform, Josiah was apprized of the discovery of "the book of the law" which had been hidden in the Temple walls (2 Kings 22:8–11). As a result of this finding, Josiah reinstated the suzerain covenant with God through the reading of the law before all the people (2 Kings 23:1–3). However, the curse against Judah for her rebellion against their Suzerain could not be reversed, but Josiah would be spared of seeing it fulfilled (2 Kings 22:15–20; cf. Deuteronomy 29:10–28).

---

3. John Bright, *A History of Israel* (Louisville: Westminister John Knox Press, 2000), pp. 312-313.

15

Desperate Attempts at Political Stability

During Josiah's reign, Assyrian domination of the Near East was crumbling from internal political intrigue and over-extension of its military powers. When Egypt began to push from the west for supremacy in Palestine, Judah was once again caught in the middle. Josiah died in battle defending the remnants of Judah from Pharaoh Neco, who was attempting to bring Judah under his subjugation. The next three kings of Judah, Jehoahaz, Jehoiakim, and Jehoiachin, either as vassals or captives, fell into the hands of the rising power of the Chaldeans pouring down upon them from the east.

Mattaniah, the sole remaining son of Josiah (later named Zedekiah by Nebuchadnezzar), was only a puppet to Babylon. In a miscalculated attempt at freedom, he formed an alliance with Egypt. In the suzerain treaty, it is the vassal who made the oath of obedience to the stipulations of the treaty (from the lesser individual to the greater), and the suzerain treaty invariably contained curses against the vassal for violation through disobedience or rebellion against the contract stipulations.

Zedekiah broke his suzerain contract with Nebuchadnezzar when he formed an alliance with Egypt, and God condemned Zedekiah for his rebellion (Ezekiel 17:11–21). Going to Egypt violated several stipulations of the suzerain contract and revealed a rebellious, untrustworthy and treacherous heart. Nebuchadnezzar recognized Zedekiah's alliance with Egypt as a declaration of enmity against the suzerain contract he had made with him, and promptly invaded Judah (Jeremiah 34:1–3).

In 587 BC, king Zedekiah was taken into captivity during the final siege against Jerusalem by Nebuchadnezzar's army. "Zedekiah with some of his soldiers fled in the night toward the Jordan (2 Kings 25:3ff.; Jeremiah 52:7ff.), no doubt hoping to reach temporary safety in Ammon, only to be overhauled near Jericho and brought before Nebuchadnezzar at his headquarters at Riblah in central Syria. He was shown no mercy. Having witnessed the execution of his sons, he was blinded and taken in chains to Babylon, where he died (2 Kings 25:6ff.; Jeremiah 52:9–11). A month later (2 Kings 25:8–12; Jeremiah 52:12–16) Nebuzaradan, commander of Nebuchadnezzar's guard, arrived in Jerusalem and, acting on orders, put the city to the torch and leveled its walls."[1]

Through all of its turbulent history, God constantly brought covenant lawsuit against His rebellious people for breaking the stipulations of the suzerain covenant they made with Him at Sinai. Though He used it, there were differences in God's suzerain covenant with Israel and the world's form of suzerain contract. These differences were based on His promise to Abraham. God used the suzerain covenant as a way to make the people accountable to Him, to bring them back to remembering His promises to Abraham. Deuteronomy is replete with His pleadings to the children of Israel "to love the LORD with all thine heart" as their father Abraham had done. It had ever been God's desire to bring Israel to full restoration of the blessings of His everlasting covenant—the one He had made with Adam, Abraham, Isaac and Jacob. The suzerain contract formula was used only because of the hardness of their hearts. God always wanted better for them.

Why did God allow this? For one reason: knowing that the people were ignorant of their true condition, God accepted the promise of the people at Sinai in an effort to get them to see their arrogance and inability to perform as promised. By showing them all the good things He wanted for His children which they couldn't do for themselves, He hoped to bring them to contrition and humility in appreciation of His gifts. God brought them to Sinai to enter into a marriage covenant, but they failed to appreciate His great love for them.

Standing at the foot of Sinai, in their immature affection for Him, they promised the LORD obedience little knowing the true condition of their hearts. However, when Israel began making contracts with other nations it showed their true character, lack of interest and devotion to God. The children of Israel had shown themselves to be dishonest in their covenant with God. Truly did the Lord speak: "Ye hypocrites, well did Esaias prophesy of you, saying, This people draweth nigh unto Me with their mouth, and honoureth Me with their lips; but their heart is far from Me." (Matthew 15:7, 8).

---

1. John Bright, *A History of Israel* (Louisville: Westminister John Knox Press, 2000), pp. 330.

16

Covenant Lawsuit Proclaimed

God allowed the children of Israel to go into captivity for repeated transgression of the stipulations of the suzerain covenant they made with Him before entering Canaan. In addition, they had never learned to appreciate the covenant He had made with their fathers Abraham, Isaac, and Jacob, which was the foundation for their acquisition of the Promised Land. God called them to task over this breach of contract.

> And the LORD said unto me, A conspiracy [an illegal alliance] is found among the men of Judah, and among the inhabitants of Jerusalem. They are turned back to the iniquities of their forefathers, which refused to hear My words; and they went after other gods to serve them: the house of Israel and the house of Judah have broken My covenant which I made with their fathers (Jeremiah 11:9, 10; 31:21).

Characterizing the national religious attitude, Zedekiah proved himself unfaithful and deceitful in his political covenant with Nebuchadnezzar. Had he remained trustworthy in his promises to Nebuchadnezzar, he might not have been taken into captivity. Because of his breach of contract, he and Judah were denounced by God for their rebellion.

> Moreover the word of the LORD came unto me, saying, Say now to the rebellious house, Know ye not what these things mean? tell them, Behold, the king of Babylon is come to Jerusalem, and hath taken the king thereof, and the princes thereof, and led them with him to Babylon; and hath taken of the king's seed, and made a covenant with him, and hath taken

an oath of him: he hath also taken the mighty of the land: that the kingdom might be base, that it might not lift itself up, but that by keeping of his covenant it might stand. But he rebelled against him in sending his ambassadors into Egypt, that they might give him horses and much people. Shall he prosper? shall he escape that doeth such things? or shall he break the covenant, and be delivered?

As I live, saith the Lord GOD, surely in the place where the king dwelleth that made him king, whose oath he despised, and whose covenant he brake, even with him in the midst of Babylon he shall die. Neither shall Pharaoh with his mighty army and great company make for him in the war, by casting up mounts, and building forts, to cut off many persons: seeing he despised the oath by breaking the covenant, when, lo, he had given his hand, and hath done all these things, he shall not escape (Ezekiel 17:11–18).

The nation of Israel had proven that they could not be honest in their dealings with men or with God. In Ezekiel 17:19, 20, God mentions both His covenant with Abraham (His oath) and the covenant He entered into at Sinai as being broken by the rebellious nation. Covenant lawsuit brought imprisonment for the lawbreakers, that they might learn repentance.

Therefore thus saith the Lord GOD; as I live, surely Mine oath that he hath despised, and My covenant that he hath broken, even it will I recompense upon his own head. And I will spread My net upon him, and he shall be taken in My snare, and I will bring him to Babylon, and will plead with him there for his trespass that he hath trespassed against Me (Ezekiel 17:19, 20).

We must take note of the distinction between the oath of God and covenant of men. When God made His covenant with Abraham (Genesis 15:9–21), He made a solemn promise to His faithful servant swearing that He would give him a land for his perpetual inheritance. God's eternal promise to save His people from their sin can never be broken; it is as sure and solid as His character. However, the promises and pledges of men are as unstable as water.

In this verse, God says that Israel never believed His promise to Abraham (the oath), nor did they keep their pledge of obedience made at Sinai (the covenant). On both counts, they were guilty. In these instances the covenant between God and Israel was a conditional covenant—"if you do certain things, then I will do certain things"—and appears as such throughout the Old Testament (e.g. Exodus 19:5, 6; 23:20–25; Leviticus 26:3; Deuteronomy 6:17. "If" and "then" are implied in the statement, see Isaiah 1:18; Jeremiah 4:1; Jeremiah 12:16).

In what took place at Sinai and especially Deuteronomy chapters 28 and 29, we find parallels to the ancient suzerain contract, in which the suzerain promised certain things if the people lived up to the stipulations of the contract; blessings for obedience and curses for rebellion. But this form of covenant was not God's intended method for His everlasting covenant. It's use was made necessary because of the faithless obstinance of the people, and so they were called "stiffnecked and uncircumcised in heart and ears," a people who had "always resist[ed] the Holy Ghost: as your fathers did, so do ye." (Acts 7:51, cf. Exodus 32:9; 33:3, 5; 34:9; Deuteronomy 9:6, 13; 31:27; Nehemiah 9:16; etc.).

In a withering denunciation of her unstable character, God condemned Judah not only for breaking the covenants she had repeatedly made with foreign nations, but also for her whoredoms against His covenant with her. Israel repeatedly refused to live up to her agreement with God, and refused to believe God's promise to her (Isaiah 1:2–15; 24:5), thus provoking the Lord to bring a covenant lawsuit against His people.

> Thou hast also committed fornication with the Egyptians thy neighbors, great of flesh; and hast increased thy whoredoms, to provoke Me to anger. Behold, therefore I have stretched out My hand over thee, and have diminished thine ordinary food, and delivered thee unto the will of them that hate thee, the daughters of the Philistines, which are ashamed of thy lewd way. Thou hast played the whore also with the Assyrians, because thou wast unsatiable; yea, thou hast played the harlot with them, and yet couldest not be satisfied.[1] Thou hast moreover multiplied thy fornication in the land of Canaan unto Chaldea; and yet thou wast not satisfied herewith.
>
> How weak is thine heart, saith the Lord GOD, seeing thou doest all these things, the work of an imperious whorish woman; in that thou buildest thine eminent place in the head

---

1. Whoredom and harlotry are words describing sexual impurity indicating breakage of the marriage covenant.

of every way, and makest thine high place in every street; and hast not been as an harlot, in that thou scornest hire; but as a wife that committeth adultery, which taketh strangers instead of her husband! (Ezekiel 16:26–32; see also vv. 22–43).

As the remnants of Israel were being carted off to Babylon, God declared:—

Behold, the days come, saith the LORD, that I will make a new covenant with the house of Israel, and with the house of Judah: not according to the covenant that I made with their fathers in the day that I took them by the hand to bring them out of the land of Egypt; which My covenant they brake, although I was an husband unto them, saith the LORD: but this shall be the covenant that I will make with the house of Israel; after those days, saith the LORD, I will put My law in their inward parts, and write it in their hearts; and will be their God, and they shall be My people. And they shall teach no more every man his neighbor, and every man his brother, saying, know the LORD: for they shall all know Me, from the least of them unto the greatest of them, saith the LORD: for I will forgive their iniquity, and I will remember their sin no more (Jeremiah 31:31–34).

The object of God's everlasting covenant is always a spiritual commitment between Himself and His people. It is *not* limited to a single race, tribe, denomination, or congregation. Both Paul and Peter in their letters to Gentile converts referred to these non-descendants of Abraham as "heirs according to the promise." (Galatians 3:28, 29; see also Romans 2:28, 29; Philippians 3:3; Ephesians 1:4, 5, 7). Ethnic "Jews" could only become part of the covenant promise by faith in the Messiah (Romans 9:6-8, 25-33).

This is the way it has always been, from the foundation of the world. Adam received the promise of the Messiah (Genesis 3:15), through faith in God's promise. Abraham "looked for a city which hath foundations, whose builder and maker is God," and was "counted righteous" (Hebrews 11:10; Genesis 15:6; Romans 4:3, 13–17). Writing to the Gentile converts in Asia minor, Peter counts them all as a "chosen generation, a royal priesthood, an holy nation, a peculiar people" repeating the words of God to Israel at Sinai (Exodus 19:5, 6). The everlasting covenant is God's promise to save the world, Jew and Gentile, through Jesus Christ. Without faith in Christ as his Saviour, no ethnic Jew or any nation today can hope of any special privileges from God.

The suzerain covenant He had made with Israel at Sinai was not the one He desired to make with them. That covenant was a defective covenant, based on the faulty promises of the people (Hebrews 8:7–12). God desired to write His covenant on His people's soft, pliant hearts, just as He had done with Abraham, Isaac, and Jacob. He's still awaiting His opportunity, when spiritual Israel will finally heed the counsel of the True Witness (Revelation 3:14–22).

Persistence of the Vassal Mentality

Even while He was sending them into captivity, God was planning His people's redemption.

> Therefore fear thou not, O my servant Jacob, saith the LORD; neither be dismayed, O Israel: for, lo, I will save thee from afar, and thy seed from the land of their captivity; and Jacob shall return, and shall be in rest, and be quiet, and none shall make him afraid. For I am with thee, saith the LORD, to save thee: though I make a full end of all nations whither I have scattered thee, yet will I not make a full end of thee: but I will correct thee in measure, and will not leave thee altogether unpunished (Jeremiah 30:10, 11).

Continuing with his good news, Jeremiah announced: "The LORD hath appeared unto me, saying, Yea, I have loved thee with an everlasting love: therefore with lovingkindness have I drawn thee" (Jeremiah 31:3).

On their return from Babylon the children of Israel took up where they left off, a bit more subdued perhaps, but still thinking like a vassal. Reviewing their history to them, Nehemiah praised God for His faithfulness to His promise to Abraham in delivering the children of Israel to the Promised Land (Nehemiah 9:7, 8). He recounted the protection and provision God had given to the infant nation, but was honest in his reiteration of their sordid history; they were only evil continually.

> Many times didst Thou deliver them according to Thy mercies; and testifiedst against them, that Thou mightest bring them again unto Thy law: yet they dealt proudly, and hearkened not unto Thy commandments, but sinned against Thy judgments, (which if a man do, he shall live in them;) and withdrew the shoulder, and hardened their neck, and would not hear (Nehemiah 9:29).

At the end of his discourse, Nehemiah and the people again made a solemn vow before the Lord promising God to be obedient. "And because of all this we make a sure covenant, and write it; and our princes, Levites, and priests, seal unto it" (v. 38).

Having learned their lessons about covenanting with the surrounding nations, Israel set about to isolate themselves from temptation. They not only built walls around their cities, but around their dealings with men in general, hedging themselves in by erecting a wall of partition that would remain until the coming of Christ.

> The effort to earn salvation by one's own works inevitably leads men to pile up human exactions as a barrier against sin. For, seeing that they fail to keep the law, they will devise rules and regulations of their own to force themselves to obey. All this turns the mind away from God to self. His love dies out of the heart, and with it perishes love for his fellow men.[2]

Israel never got past seeing God other than in relationship to law—do's and don't's—that they thought pleased Him. Never could they see that He was trying to teach them fidelity, loyalty, responsibility, and true devotion. They remained in their vassal-slave mentality, never recognizing God as the loving, kind, and merciful One that He is.

When He appeared on earth as their Saviour, their vassal mentality led them to reject and crucify their LORD. Tragically, the freedom He spoke about, they could not comprehend, preferring their bondage to the law which condemned them. To the leadership of the church, the teaching of Jesus was antinomian and opposed to everything in which they had trust and confidence.

> Israel had not perceived the spiritual nature of the law, and too often their professed obedience was but an observance of forms and ceremonies, rather than a surrender of the heart to the sovereignty of love. As Jesus in His character and work represented to men the holy, benevolent, and paternal attributes of God, and presented the worthlessness of mere ceremonial obedience, the Jewish leaders did not receive or understand His words.[3]

---

2. Ellen G. White, *Thoughts from the Mount of Blessing* (Bosie: Pacific Press, 1955), p. 123.
3. Ibid., p. 46.

[Jesus] declared that the righteousness upon which the Pharisees set so great value was worthless. The Jewish nation had claimed to be the special, loyal people who were favored of God; but Christ represented their religion as devoid of saving faith. All their pretensions of piety, their human inventions and ceremonies, and even their boasted performance of the outward requirements of the law, could not avail to make them holy. They were not pure in heart or noble and Christlike in character.

A legal religion is insufficient to bring the soul into harmony with God. The hard, rigid orthodoxy of the Pharisees, destitute of contrition, tenderness, or love, was only a stumbling block to sinners. ...

The prophet Hosea had pointed out what constitutes the very essence of Pharisaism, in the words, "Israel is an empty vine, he bringeth forth fruit unto himself." Hosea 10:1. In their professed service to God, the Jews were really working for self. Their righteousness was the fruit of their own efforts to keep the law according to their own ideas and for their own selfish benefit. Hence it could be no better than they were. In their endeavor to make themselves holy, they were trying to bring a clean thing out of an unclean. The law of God is as holy as He is holy, as perfect as He is perfect. It presents to men the righteousness of God. It is impossible for man, of himself, to keep this law; for the nature of man is depraved, deformed, and wholly unlike the character of God. The works of the selfish heart are "as an unclean thing;" and "all our righteousnesses are as filthy rags." Isaiah 64:6.[4]

The spirit of Phariseeism is the spirit of human nature. It dogged Israel just as much as it tenaciously clings to all of us today.

The record is clear. The covenant the people had promised to keep while standing at the foot of Sinai was only sporadically kept, if at all. Our LORD's wistful comment is sadly proven to be true, "O that there were such an heart in them, that they would fear Me, and keep all My commandments always, that it might be well with them, and with their children for ever!" (Deuteronomy 5:28-29).

---

4. Ibid., pp. 53-54.

Part IV

God's Everlasting Covenant

17

Original Objective for the Exodus from Egypt

God's original plan for His children was that they would remember the covenant He had previously made with their fathers, Abraham, Isaac, and Jacob, which included the promise of an inheritance and a conveyance of land (Genesis 15:13–21; 26:2–5; 28:1–4; 28:10–15). He remembered it. "God remembered His covenant with Abraham, Isaac, and Jacob" (Exodus 2:24), and He repeatedly referred to it all through the first section of the Exodus narrative. "And I am come down to deliver them out of the hand of the Egyptians, and to bring them up out of that land unto a good land and a large, unto a land flowing with milk and honey; unto the place of the Canaanites, and the Hittites, and the Amorites, and the Perizzites, and the Hivites, and the Jebusites." (Exodus 3:8, cf. Genesis 15:18–21).

When Moses hesitated under God's command to return to Egypt as His spokesman, God used the divine identifier consisting of the phrase "The LORD God of your fathers, Abraham, Isaac, and Jacob," thus tying His identity to His covenant with the patriarchs. Further, God then instructed Moses on how to approach his people back home in Egypt. He told him to say unto them:—

> The LORD God of your fathers, *of Abraham, of Isaac, and of Jacob*, appeared unto me, saying I have surely visited you, and seen that which is done to you in Egypt. And I have said, I will bring you up out of the affliction of Egypt unto the land of the Canaanites, and the Hittites, and the Amorites, and the Perizzites, and the Hivites, and the Jebusites, unto a land flowing with milk and honey (vss. 16, 17, emphasis supplied).

This was a direct reference to the dying words of Joseph that had been handed down generation to generation: "And Joseph said unto his brethren, I die: and God will surely visit you, and bring you out of this land unto the land which He sware *to Abraham, to Isaac, and to Jacob*" (Genesis 50:24, emphasis supplied).

Why did God place such strong emphasis on the fact that He was the God of Abraham, Isaac, and Jacob? Because the everlasting covenant was integrally bound to the promise given to these patriarchs. The covenant made with the patriarchs was the same covenant that God was now attempting to revive with their descendants.

After Pharaoh increased the burden upon the Israelites, Moses complained to God that He had not yet delivered His people as He had promised (Exodus 5:23). Patiently, God reaffirms His purpose by declaring His name, followed with His intent to renew the covenant made with Abraham, Isaac, and Jacob. Eternally bracketed between the beginning and ending declarations that He is God (there is none like unto Him), He said:—

> I am the LORD: and I appeared unto Abraham, unto Isaac, and unto Jacob, by the name of God Almighty, but by My name JEHOVAH was I not known to them. And I have also established My covenant with them, to give them the land of Canaan, the land of their pilgrimage, wherein they were strangers. And I have also heard the groaning of the children of Israel, whom the Egyptians keep in bondage; and I have remembered My covenant.
>
> Wherefore say unto the children of Israel, I am the LORD, and I will bring you out from under the burdens of the Egyptians, and I will rid you out of their bondage, and I will redeem you with a stretched out arm, and with great judgments: and I will take you to Me for a people, and I will be to you a God: and ye shall know that I am the LORD your God, which bringeth you out from under the burdens of the Egyptians. And I will bring you in unto the land, concerning the which I did swear to give it to Abraham, to Isaac, and to Jacob; and I will give it you for an heritage: I am the LORD (Exodus 6:2–8; cf. 3:7–17).

Five times, God emphasizes the fact that He is God—the eternal, unchanging, dynamic, ever present, absolute Being. He said "I have established My covenant" and "I have remembered My covenant." Then He explains what the covenant is all about: I will deliver you from your burdens, from your bondage, and I will redeem you. Then I will take you to be My special people and deliver you into the land that I promised to your fathers, Abraham, Isaac, and Jacob, and I will be your God forever, and through it all "I will be with you" (Hebrew *'ehyeh*, cf. Exodus 3:12, 14) assuring you of divine protection. In this multifaceted promise are included several specific blessings—(1) intimate knowledge of their Redeemer, (2) the establishment of a community of believers who were intended to be His witnesses, and (3) rest from their bondage. In essence, God is everything this poor people need, now and forever. What more could they ask for?

Did God know the needs of the people? "And God heard their groaning, and God remembered His covenant with Abraham, with Isaac, and with Jacob. And God looked upon the children of Israel, and God had respect unto them." (Exodus 2:24, 25). God remembered His covenant with Abraham, Isaac and Jacob—the everlasting covenant. Unlike Biblical references to pagan gods, these verses contain active verbs which reveal a personal God who participates in the lives of His people: God heard, God remembered, God looked, and God knew or had knowledge of their condition and needs (literal meaning of the Hebrew *yadà*).

As was previously discussed, this was a lesson the Israelites never learned. Only twice in the entire Exodus narrative do we find any intimation that the Israelites have the competency to appreciate God's promise to them. When Moses and Aaron worked God's miracles before the unbelieving crowds,[1] "the people believed: and when they heard that the LORD had visited the children of Israel, and that He had looked upon their affliction, then they bowed their heads and worshipped" (Exodus

---

1. "The signs which will be executed in Egypt, possess a distinctly Egyptian coloration. This is not surprising, for magic was a pervasive ingredient of everyday life in Egypt, deeply embedded in the culture. The signs taught to Moses are intended, first and foremost, to validate his claim to be the divinely chosen instrument for the redemption of Israel. On a secondary level, they also function to establish the superiority of Moses over the Egyptian magicians and, by extension to affirm the superior might of Israel's God over those who the Egyptians worshiped as gods. Moses, however, is not a magician. He possesses no superhuman powers and no esoteric knowledge; he is unable to initiate or perform anything except by precise instructions from God; he pronounces no spells, observes no rituals, and employs no occult techniques, and often he does not know in advance the consequences of the actions he is told to perform." Nahum M. Sarna, *The JPS Torah Commentary* (New York: Jewish Publication Society, 1991), p. 20.

4:31, Genesis 50:24). After the miracle of the Red Sea deliverance, the people again "believed the LORD" (Exodus 14:31). Both of these were superficial conversions as evidenced by the speed with which the people resumed their murmuring against their merciful and longsuffering God (Exodus 5:20, 21; 15:23–26).

The first was predicated on their hope of reward. The second was couched in their fear of this awesome God who could turn water into blood, cause masses of frogs, lice, flies and locusts to burst from thin air, cause disease on beasts and humans, simultaneously rain hail and fire from the sky, take or preserve life at His will, and now He stood water up like a wall of stone, allowing them passage on dry ground. There was no god like this among all the pantheon of Egypt!

Oh yes, they knew about God, but had no personal experiential knowledge of Him. Their lack of knowing reduced their energy to serve Him as their only source of salvation. It quashed their ability to boldly proclaim Him as the Saviour of the world, and kept hidden from them the contentment and rest which comes only through being completely yielded and still in His love.

As a result, in the three months it took for them to travel to Sinai, they were no closer to developing a true appreciation of God's character than before Moses returned to call them from their bondage. Repeatedly, they exhibited their unbelief in God's power to protect them and provide for their every need. When they heard the words of the LORD directing them to remember (again!) the covenant He had made with their fathers, Abraham, Isaac, and Jacob, their unbelief led them to make an impetuous promise that they could never hope to keep, thus bringing them into bondage (Exodus 19:8; Galatians 4:24, 25). They thwarted God's plans to make them a free people in the land of promise; a people who could be a true witness for Him of His power to save from sin to the uttermost.

When the children of Israel were standing on the edge of the Promised Land, Moses reminded them that they were only obtaining the promised inheritance because God was faithful to His oath. They had done absolutely nothing to deserve what they were receiving.

> Not for thy righteousness, or for the uprightness of thine heart, dost thou go to possess their land: but for the wickedness of these nations the LORD thy God doth drive them out from before thee, and that He may perform the word which the LORD sware unto thy fathers, Abraham, Isaac, and Jacob. Understand therefore, that the LORD thy God giveth thee not this good land

to possess it for thy righteousness; for thou art a stiffnecked people (Deuteronomy 9:5).[2]

The Israelites were never able to experience the true motivation which springs from a true heart appreciation of the unselfish, redemptive love of God, nor develop an authentic allegiance to Him. The friendship with God that Abraham, Isaac, and Jacob had experienced, remained elusive. Instead, they constantly operated from a sense of contractual obligation, which is legalism and old covenantism. Their unwillingness to yield up their preconceived opinions about His character frustrated God's original intentions for His people. His sole desire was to renew His everlasting covenant with them, and to make them "a peculiar treasure unto [Him] above all people ... to make [them] a kingdom of priests and a holy nation" that would demonstrate a true witness of His character before all the world.

---

2. See also Deuteronomy 1:8; 6:18; 8:1; 11:9; 11:21; 26:3; 28:11; 30:20; and Joshua 5:6. In each of these verses we find the phrase "which the LORD sware" referring to the oath given to Abraham in Genesis 15:18; cf. Hebrews 6:16-18. The children of Israel only obtained the inheritance by *promise* from God, not by anything they did or could have done.

18

Royal Land Grant Treaty as the Formula for the Everlasting Covenant

Running throughout the first section of the Exodus narrative is the constantly repeated subject of land as a part of the covenant promise to Abraham. Paralleling God's covenant to Abraham, we find ancient Near Eastern covenants conveying land by royal decree to favored vassals. The suzerain covenant is similar to the land grant in legal linguistic form, however, the royal land grant had some major differences which we will examine in this section of our study.

To a large extent, the focus of the Bible's message is about land and the right of inheritance to that land. In both the Old and New Testaments, we find a recurring motif of land lost and redeemed, of a people in exile and then returned to their homeland, from Eden lost to Eden restored.

> The symbol of land is universalized when Paul speaks of the promise to Abraham and his descendants that they would 'inherit the world' (Romans 4:13). And the pattern of exodus followed by possession of the land is echoed in Christ having 'delivered us from the dominion of darkness' and 'qualified us to share in the inheritance of the saints in light' (Colossians 1:12, 13).[1]

This central theme of land is founded in the grant of land bestowed by God in covenant promise to His creatures beginning in Genesis chapter one, restated with an expanded definition to Abraham in Genesis chapters 12 through 17, and then reconfirmed to David in 2 Samuel 7.

Before undertaking an analysis of the royal grant covenant formula, an understanding of "the fundamental concepts and distinctions

---

1. Leland Ryken, James C. Wilhoit and Tremper Longman, III, eds., *Dictionary of Biblical Imagery* (Downers Grove, Ill.: InterVarsity Press, 1998), p. 488.

between contract and real property law will prove helpful. Both contract and property have been foundational virtually to all ordered societies throughout recorded history. While refined over the centuries, the essential rules of both contract and property law have remained for the most part constant. Therefore, even contemporary articulations of these legal themes provide a valid definitional basis for consideration of ancient judicial formulae."[2]

In his study, "Legal Models for the Old Testament Covenants," Cordell P. Schulten, using the definition found in the American Law Institute's "Restatement (Second) of Contracts," says: "A contract is a promise or a set of promises for the breach of which the law gives a remedy or the performance of which the law in some way recognizes a duty." Contrary to this is the royal land grant, based on real property law. "While contract is founded upon promise, property law is based upon right, or more accurately, a bundle of rights. … The grant of rights in the land derived from the sovereignty of the king. The rights granted included title (i.e. ownership), possession, use and alienation (i.e. the ability of the grantee to transfer his rights to others)."[3]

The extant texts describing land grants have been examined and divided into four main categories describing their purposes:—

1. Grants of land from the king to a private individual as a reward for loyalty and faithful service.
2. Grants of land from the king to private individuals made to enable the individual to provide offerings at the local temple.
3. Grants of land from the king to priests who provided service for the local temple.
4. Decrees issued by the king delineating what gifts the temple should receive and who should provide them.

In the simple form of royal grant, the king prepares a document which states that he has presented to the recipient a certain amount of property—which normally includes fields, orchards, "houses," and people—and that he has freed this property and the recipient himself from taxes. The document

---

2. Cordell P. Schulten, "Legal Models for the Old Testament Covenants, An Issue of Contract or Real property Law?" Document found on the Missouri Baptist University web site; retrieved August 12, 2003, from http://www.mobap.edu/schulten/LegalModels.OTCovenants1.htm
3. Schulten.

then closed with injunctions to later rulers, curses, and finally with the date.[4]

Taxes from which the recipient was exempt included taxation of property, taxes paid in kind, taxes on travel and transport, and exemption from compulsory labour and military service.[5] These elements resemble the pattern for the land grant we will examine illustrating the Biblical covenant made with Abraham.

The Author of the true covenant, the everlasting covenant, gives us an illustration of the royal land grant covenant in Genesis 1 and 2 (Adamic covenant), Genesis 9 (Noahic covenant), and Genesis 12, 13, 15 and 17 (Abrahamic covenant). With each patriarch, we do not find a totally new or different covenant, but a renewal and restatement of the original covenant—I AM the LORD your God, be fruitful, multiply and bless the earth, filling it with My righteousness. The possession of the land was an inherent aspect of this promise, as was the faithful acceptance of Jehovah as the one true God, the only source for the blessings that were promised to the believer. The endowment of the original property title to Adam was renewed in the Noahic covenant, and again to Abraham, with the inclusion of Messianic promises. Each restatement of the covenant is a reward for loyalty and devotion to God.[6] The recipient responded with submission and devotion to God in appreciation for the gift.[7]

God created the royal land grant; it's His own "formula" for the everlasting covenant. There exists incredible correlations between what we read in the Bible and what the nations afterward did with this form of covenant, but all nations learned it from God's example. They mirrored His covenant in the granting of lands to favored individuals. Land grants have to do with the graciousness and mercy of the sovereign toward his faithful people. The king could grant land because, in ancient times, he owned everything within his earthly realm. Such a granting of land was to be a perpetual arrangement to all the future generations of the individual to whom the land was given.

Based on the promise of the king (grantor) to the recipient (grantee), we find that the land grant was focused on the receiver of the promise,

---

4. J.N. Postgate, *Neo-Assyrian Royal Grants and Decrees* (Rome: Pontifical Biblical Institute, 1969), p. 3.

5. Postgate, pp. 9-16.

6. Moshe Weinfeld, "The Covenant of Grant in the Old Testament and in the Ancient Near East," *Essential Papers on Israel and the Ancient Near East*, Frederick E. Greenspahn, ed. (New York: New York University Press, 1991), p. 70.

7. Ibid., pp. 70-71.

not the one who did the promising (the One promising was God). Unlike the suzerain contract that was instituted for the protection of the suzerain against the revolt or treachery of his vassals, land grants were "other" centered, not self-centered. "The grant par excellence is an act of royal benevolence arising from the king's desire to reward his loyal servant. It is no wonder, then, that the gift of the Land to Abraham and the assurance of a dynasty to David were formulated in the style of grants to outstanding servants."[8]

Hittite and Syro-Palestinian political treaties often included the conveyance of land as tokens of favor from the suzerain to his vassal and the vassal's descendants. Archeological evidence exists proving that royal land grants were used extensively beginning in the second millennium BC and continuing for nearly a thousand years in the ancient Near East. "Royal land grant treaties or covenants have been found in Hittite, Babylonian and Neo-Assyrian texts and most recently in materials from Ras Shamra. They are particularly known from the Babylonian kudurru[9] or boundary stones, texts which cover a period from 1450 BC to 550 BC, i.e., the whole period of Babylonian history during which Boundary-stones were employed for the protection of private property."[10] The kudurru stones contained the description of the territory conveyed and were authenticated with the suzerain's royal seal.

While not as tightly structured as the suzerain covenant formula, the royal land grants did exhibit several unique and identifiable characteristics. Like the suzerain contracts, the grant usually contained a preamble identifying the king giving the land, an historical prologue delineating the reason for the grant, which was followed by the king's promises to the vassal. Unlike the suzerain contracts, there was no particular order for these elements, and the curses were directed, not toward the vassal, but toward anyone who would violate the privileges

---

8. Ibid., p. 72.

9. Kudurru stones were boundary markers used by the Kassites of ancient Mesopotamia. It usually consisted of a slab of rock or stone set at the boundaries of lands given via royal decree. The original kudurru were kept in temples while clay copies were given to landowners as proof of title to the land. Engraved on the stone were the clauses of the covenant, images or symbols of the gods under whose protection the gift was placed, and the curse on those who violated the rights conferred. From *Encyclopedia Britannica*, 2002 CD-ROM version.

10. Tim Hegg, "The Covenant of Grant and The Abrahamic Covenant," p. 2. A PDF version of a document read at the Regional Evangelical Theological Society, 1989. Document retrieved from the Internet on September 5, 2003.

granted by the king to the vassal. The king's seal on the document was verification that he would stand behind his promise to the vassal, protecting his rights to ownership, possession of use, and perpetuity.

1. Royal land grants bestowed land to a favored individual for faithful or loyal service to the master. The grant of Ashurbanipal to his servant Bulta was worded: "Baltya … whose heart is devoted (whole) to his master, served me (stood before me) with truthfulness, acted perfectly (walked in perfection) in my palace, grew up with a good name and kept the charge of my kingship."[11]

2. The grantee's rights to the property were guaranteed by the sovereign, with punishment promised to anyone who would infringe upon those rights. The presence of the royal seal demonstrated the sovereign's pledge of protection.

3. Royal land grants conveyed perpetual ownership to the individual and his posterity, thus setting up a dynastic succession relating to the possession of the land. The common verbiage was "he sealed it and gave it to him forever." It was intended that the behavior of the heirs would continue to follow the original recipient's loyal example. "'Land' and 'house' (= dynasty), the objects of the Abrahamic and Davidic covenants respectively, are indeed the most prominent gifts of the suzerain in the Hittite and Syro-Palestinian political reality, and like the Hittite grants so also the grant of land to Abraham and the grant of 'house' to David are unconditional."[12] The legal element of possession in perpetuity was prominent in the ancient royal grants. "Especially instructive in this case are the formulations of conveyance in perpetuity. So, for example, the formulae: 'for your descendants forever' (Genesis 15:15), 'for your descendants after you throughout your generations' (Genesis 15:7, 8), are identical with the conveyance and donation formulae from Susa, Alalah, Ugarit, and Elephantine."[13]

---

11. Weinfeld, p. 70.
12. Ibid., p. 73.
13. Ibid., p. 82.

4. The fourth element was the inclusion of the identification and title of the sovereign making the grant.

Comparing these elements to the Abrahamic covenant we find that Ashurbanipal's complimentary statements about his faithful servant echo God's words about Abraham, His own faithful servant. "And when Abram was ninety years old and nine, the Lord appeared to Abram, and said unto him, I am the Almighty God; walk before me, and be thou perfect" (Genesis 17:1). This verse also contains the preamble that identifies the sovereign and gives His title—the Almighty God—Sovereign Lord of the universe.

Land grants included a walking survey during which the kudurru stones were set in place. This correlates to God's command to Abraham to walk throughout the land, taking possession of it. Instead of erecting kudurru stones, at various places Abraham built altars to his God.

> And the Lord said unto Abram, after that Lot was separated from him, Lift up now thine eyes, and look from the place where thou art northward, and southward, and eastward, and westward: for all the land which thou seest, to thee will I give it, and to thy seed for ever. And I will make thy seed as the dust of the earth: so that if a man can number the dust of the earth, then shall thy seed also be numbered (Genesis 13:14–16).

Here God signifies the perpetuity of the covenant including the promise of children as yet unconceived who would inherit it. Abraham's name would be "great" throughout all the earth (Genesis 12:2). As the royal grant assumed, the grantee would "command his children and his household after him, and they shall keep the way of the LORD, to do justice and judgment; that the LORD may bring upon Abraham that which He hath spoken of him" (Genesis 18:19). Should anyone challenge Abraham's God-given right to the land, He personally would defend Abraham and his heir's lawful title to the royal estate (Genesis 12:3).

The gift of this world was intended to be Adam's eternal possession. It is the first instance of a royal land grant. After the creation of everything in this world, God fashioned mankind saying "let them have dominion over the fish of the sea, and over the fowl of the air, and over the cattle, and over all the earth, and over every creeping thing that creepeth upon the earth" (Genesis 1:26).

For the purposes of our study, dominion is the key word in this verse. It means the right to reign or rule over the territory given. The royal land grant included the right of the grantee to free use and control over the domain presented to him. That Adam had this right is established in the fact that God allowed Adam to name all the animals which dwelt in his domain. The "kudurru stones" were laid out in the boundary description (Genesis 2:10–14), with the one restriction, that which was reserved for the King alone, being identified in vv. 16, 17. Adam promised nothing to God in return for this gift; all he could do was receive it gladly from the hand of his Creator. In appreciation, Adam was to faithfully serve his Lord and cherish His gift (Genesis 2:15), teaching his children after him to honor the Grantor of the precious gift of life and land.

19

Legal Foundations for the Land Grant

We now need to examine a few legal definitions. They shed light on our topic supplying a valid reference for what we read in the Bible about the royal land grant. We are not defining the Bible by the law dictionary, but rather viewing the law through the lens of the Bible. God is the beginning and end of all things. God is the Sovereign Lord who owns everything and has legal right to convey anything He wishes to His loyal and faithful servants. God possesses full and clear title to the estate He granted to Adam, then to Noah, and then to Abraham and his faithful heirs. That civil law has come to embody these elements merely testifies to the universal goodness of God's promises to His people.[1]

Numerous terms are used in property law and real estate to define the activities of the covenanting parties. A term in some ways synonymous with the land grant is *seisin* covenant. *Seisin* covenant is a covenant which states that the grantor has an estate, or the right to convey an estate, of the quality and size that the grantor purports to convey. For the covenant to be valid, the grantor must have both title and possession at the time of the grant. Covenant of *seisin* usually appears as part of a warranty deed, which states that the grantor does in fact have both the title to and legal possession of an estate or property, and possesses the right to convey that holding to a grantee. Warranty deed includes the covenant by which the grantor in a deed promises to secure to the grantee the estate conveyed in the deed, and pledges to defend the

---

1. For nearly a millennium the British monarchy has utilized the "land grant" concept to distribute land to men faithful to the Crown. To this day the British monarchy has maintained the right of dukes, marquesses, earls, viscounts, and barons to inherit title and land. These noblemen constitute the house of lords.

grantee against any unlawful or unreasonable claims of superior title made by a third party, to indemnify the grantee for any loss sustained by the third party claim, and to compensate the grantee with other land if the grantee is evicted by someone having better title to the property. This type of covenant is binding on all the grantor's heirs.[2]

Under certain circumstances, property bestowed under a royal land grant could be lost or divested—the possession, or right of occupancy to the property could be presumed by a usurper. In such cases, only an "abstract right" to the property was in effect until such time as it could be redeemed. This situation is termed "mere right." "A person in this situation may have the true and ultimate property of the lands in himself, but the intervention of certain circumstances, either by his own negligence, the solemn act of his ancestor, or the determination of a court of justice, the presumptive evidence of that right is strongly in favor of his antagonist, who has thereby obtained the absolute right of possession. The heir therefore in this case has only a mere right, and must be strictly held to the proof of it, in order to recover the lands."[3]

Through their "own negligence" the ethnic Jews forfeited their rights to their ancestral lands in Palestine when they crucified their Redeemer, and persistently rejected the continued witness to them through Christ's followers (Acts 7:51–58; Matthew 23:33–38). The stoning of Stephen marked the end of their probation as a nation, fulfilling the prophecy of Daniel 9:24–27. After AD 70, the destruction of Jerusalem and their dispersion throughout the world,[4] Jews only possess a "mere right" (see *Black's Law Dictionary*) that must be proven through the heavenly courts when, individually, they confess true faith in Jesus Christ as their Saviour. Only in this way can an ethnic Jew become an "heir" of the covenant promise whose executor/mediator is Jesus Christ (Hebrews 9:15).

> Now to Abraham and his seed were the promises made.
> He saith not, And to seeds, as of many; but as of one, And to

---

2. Bryan A. Garner, ed., *Blacks Law Dictionary* (St. Paul, Minn.: West Group, 1999), pp. 371 and 1581.

3. Garner, p. 1002.

4. See Leviticus 26:28–39. In the language of a suzerain contract, Moses began the reiteration of God's curse concerning disobedience by saying: "I call heaven and earth to witness against you this day" Deuteronomy 4:26–29. God promised that if Israel remained unfaithful to Him, continued in their rejection of His everlasting covenant which is focused on Jesus Christ, Saviour of the world, then He would reject them as a nation and disperse them among all the nations of the world. This was fulfilled in AD 70 when Jerusalem was destroyed by Rome.

thy seed, which is Christ. ... And if ye be Christ's, then are ye Abraham's seed, and heirs according to the promise (Galatians 3:16, 29).

Not as though the word of God hath taken none effect. For they are not all Israel, which are of Israel: neither, because they are the seed of Abraham, are they all children: but, In Isaac shall thy seed be called. That is, They which are the children of the flesh, these are not the children of God: but the children of the promise are counted for the seed. For this is the word of promise, At this time will I come, and Sara shall have a son. And not only this; but when Rebecca also had conceived by one, even by our father Isaac; (for the children being not yet born, neither having done any good or evil, that the purpose of God according to election might stand, not of works, but of him that calleth;) it was said unto her, The elder shall serve the younger. As it is written, Jacob have I loved, but Esau have I hated. What shall we say then? Is there unrighteousness with God? God forbid. For he saith to Moses, I will have mercy on whom I will have mercy, and I will have compassion on whom I will have compassion. So then it is not of him that willeth, nor of him that runneth, but of God that sheweth mercy (Romans 9:6–16).

Through the temptation and fall of Adam, control of this world and everything in it has been transferred to Satan, who is now called the "prince of this world" (see John 12:31; and 16:11; Job 1:7; 1 Peter 5:8, etc.). After the fall, Adam and his posterity possessed only a mere right to the inheritance granted to them from the foundation of the world. Satan, through the power of sin and death, assumed dominion over the earth. Satan made boast of his possession and control of this world when he attended the grand council meeting in heaven. When God asked him to declare which territory he was representing, Satan arrogantly said he had placed his foot on every part of the earth; it was his property by right of possession and walking survey (Job 1:7).

Adam lost his inheritance when he sinned and forfeited to Satan his birthright possession of the land. He and his family retained only a mere right of possession in it until such time as it could be redeemed for them by Someone who could provide the positive proof of a clear, unencumbered title.

The story of Ruth offers insights into this process both as a legal procedure between humans, and as the pattern for the Gospel's message about our redemption and repatriation in the kingdom of God. With His blood, Christ paid for our sins, paid the full redemption price, bought back this earth, and eventually will restore it to its rightful owner and his family—Adam and his righteous posterity. Christ is the "earnest" or surety of our future possession of the inheritance first given freely to Adam, then promised freely to Abraham. An "earnest" is a token or a pledge of something that is to come in the future. The restoration of the inheritance could only come through the promised Seed (Genesis 3:15).

In Ephesians 1:3–14 the apostle Paul outlines the precious promises of the everlasting covenant of God. These promises include the free gift of the righteousness necessary to inherit the new earth. Salvation from sin and an inheritance with Christ is also included in the inheritance of the earth made new. Paul tells us that Christ is the earnest of our inheritance until the redemption of the purchased possession becomes a reality (verse 14).

- In Christ, we receive all the promises that are to come to God's faithful children.
- In Christ, we have full redemption from sin.
- In Christ, we become adopted sons and daughters of God.[5]
- In Christ, we obtain an inheritance.
- In Christ, we receive all things in heaven and earth.
- In Christ, all that was promised to Abraham is ours.

The inheritance belongs to all who are children of God through faith in Christ Jesus (Galatians 3:26-29). Those who believe in Christ's glorious deliverance from the curse of the law—which is disobedience[6]—can realize the power and blessings of the world to come. The Gospel of salvation was preached to Abraham. Abraham believed what God said

---

5. In the land grant covenants, "the phrase *I will be his father and he shall be my son* is an adoption formula and actually serves as the judicial basis for the gift of the eternal dynasty. This comes to the fore in Psalm 2 where we read: He (God) said to me: you are My son, this day have I begotten you. Ask Me and I will give you nations for your patrimony and the ends of the earth for your possession (vv. 7, 8)." Weinfeld, p. 74. See also Psalm 89 for a similar statement of adoption and protection.

6. E. J. Waggoner, *The Glad Tidings*, p. 61: "The curse, as we have seen, is *disobedience*: Cursed is everyone who does *not* abide by all things written in the book of the law, and do them. Therefore Christ has redeemed us from *disobedience* to the law." (emphasis in original).

and he received the blessing of righteousness (Genesis 15:6; Romans 4:3; Galatians 3:6). All who believe are blessed with faithful Abraham and become heirs of the promises made to Abraham (Romans 4:13–16; Galatians 3:6–9). The promise to us is the very same promise made to Abraham—the everlasting covenant.

Part V

Covenant of Grace

20

Land Grant Formula Defines Abrahamic Covenant of Grace[1]

The Abrahamic land grant is introduced in Genesis 12:1–3, expanded in Genesis 13:14–17, clarified and signified in Genesis 15.

Now the LORD had said unto Abram, Get thee out of thy country, and from thy kindred, and from thy father's house, unto a land that I will shew thee: and I will make of thee a great nation, and I will bless thee, and make thy name great; and thou shalt be a blessing: and I will bless them that bless thee, and curse him that curseth thee: and in thee shall all families of the earth be blessed (Genesis 12:1–3).

The Abrahamic covenant is not so labeled until Genesis 15:18. In this introit of Genesis 12:1–3, all of the elements of the covenant are present. It functions as a prelude, each motif given in succinct fashion, awaiting embellishment and enlargement in the subsequent texts. Interestingly, the whole covenant

---

1. "If it were not possible for us to keep the commandments of God, we should all be lost. But under the Abrahamic covenant, the covenant of grace, every provision for salvation has been made. By grace ye are saved. For as many as received him, to them gave he power to become the sons of God." (Ellen G. White, "Obedience the Fruit of Love," *Signs of the Times*, April 24, 1893).

"The spirit of bondage is engendered by seeking to live in accordance with legal religion, through striving to fulfill the claims of the law in our own strength. There is hope for us only as we come under the Abrahamic covenant, which is the covenant of grace by faith in Christ Jesus. The gospel preached to Abraham, through which he had hope, was the same gospel that is preached to us today, through which we have hope. Abraham looked unto Jesus, who is also the Author and the Finisher of our faith." (*Youths Instructor*, September 22, 1892).

section begins with Abraham going to possess a granted parcel of land in a foreign country.[2]

"Then He said unto him, 'I am the LORD who brought you out from Ur of the Chaldeans to assign this land to you as a possession." This declaration forms the preamble to the promise that was to follow, identifying the Grantor and indicating His purpose. Just as with the covenant at Sinai, the preamble identifies God as the source of the blessings. When Abraham showed confusion regarding the "how" of the fulfillment of the promised seed, God responded with a solemn oath to the patriarch (Genesis 15:1–21).

> God contracts a solemn covenant with the patriarch, who becomes the passive beneficiary of His unilateral obligation, unconditionally assumed. It would seem that this form of covenant was modeled after the royal land-grant treaty common in the ancient Near East. By this instrument a king bestows a gift of land on an individual or vassal as a reward for loyal service. … For the first time in the history of religions, God becomes a contracting party, promising a national territory to a people yet unborn.[3]

Through the making of this covenant, literally *k-r-t berit*, God assumes full responsibility for the fulfillment of the covenant.

> The cutting of the animals is thus a form of self-imprecation in which the potential violator invokes their fate upon himself. This is confirmed in the above-cited Sfire treaty, which included the following clause: "As this calf is cut up, thus Matti'el and his nobles shall be cut up." The fate of the animal is explicitly projected upon the violator. In the case of land- grant covenants, the curse would be directed against anyone who interferes with the realization of the suzerain's promise.[4]

The Abrahamic covenant is a defining component of the Gospel, which is the promise of an everlasting possession and the righteousness to obtain it.

> Do not forget as we proceed that the covenant and the promise are the same thing, and that it conveys land, even

---

2. Hegg, p. 5.

3. Nahum M. Sarna, *The JPS Torah Commentary on Genesis* (Philadelphia: Jewish Publication Society, 1989), pp. 114-115.

4. Ibid.

the whole earth made new, to Abraham and his children [his children are spiritual descendants (see Galatians 3:28, 29)]. Remember also that since only righteousness will dwell in the new heavens and the new earth, the promise included the making righteous of all who believe. This is done in Christ, in whom the promise is confirmed.[5]

The promise to Abraham in Genesis 12:1–3 included the promise of posterity who would eventually inherit and occupy the land granted to Abraham. Through his posterity, Abraham would produce the promised Redeemer who would reverse the terrible state of affairs set in operation at the fall of Adam. "The promise to Abraham is seen as the embodiment of Yahweh's plan of redemption. As such, its unilateral nature, initially seen in its affinity to the grant treaty, is all the more emphasized. The redemptive blessing to mankind is the ultimate promise and it is guaranteed as the gift of the King."[6]

It is the covenant with Abraham that forms the background for Paul's discussion of the covenants in Galatians, Romans, and Hebrews. Abraham is portrayed as the father of the faithful; all who are Christ's are heirs according to the promise given to Abraham; through Abraham's posterity would come the Redeemer. The covenant made with Abraham is contrasted with the covenant made at Sinai, which was a covenant of bondage.

The New Testament focus is on the covenant with Abraham as the embodiment of the Gospel's message. "The New Testament writers do not leave us in doubt as to the identity of the one promise which they regard as summing up the hope of those who believe in Christ. They identify it for us as the promise that was made to Abraham when God called him, the promise that in him all the nations of the earth should be blessed."[7]

The promise of redemption and restoration is the Bible's overarching theme. The New Testament writers link it directly to the land grant covenant made with Abraham and restated to David. From the events of the birth of Christ to His death we find elements of the everlasting covenant portrayed clearly for us. When Zacharias prophesied Christ's birth, he said that the LORD remembers "His holy covenant, the oath

---

5. Waggoner, *The Glad Tidings*, p. 72.

6. Hegg, p. 7.

7. Willis Judson Beecher, *The Prophets and the Promise* (Grand Rapids, Mich.: Baker Books, 1975), pp. 180-181.

which He sware unto our father Abraham" … and He was "raising up a horn of salvation for us in the house of His servant David" (Luke 1:69–73), thus uniting two elements of the land grant covenant together in one Person.

The apostle Paul repeatedly refers to the promise God gave to Abraham, and the whole human race. "And we declare unto you glad tidings, how that the promise which was made unto the fathers [Abraham, Isaac, and Jacob], God hath fulfilled the same unto us their children, in that He hath raised up Jesus again" (Acts 13:32, 33; John 12:32).

Paul told the Galatians that the covenant made at Sinai could not nullify the establishment of the eternal and everlasting covenant God and Christ had made with Abraham 430 years before. "And this I say, that the covenant, that was confirmed before of God in Christ, the law, which was four hundred and thirty years after, cannot disannul, that it should make the promise of none effect. For if the inheritance be of the law, it is no more of promise: but God gave it to Abraham by promise" (Galatians 3:17, 18). The inheritance comes to us only through God's promise to redeem from sin and make us righteous. This includes creating in us a new heart (Psalm 51:10; 1 Timothy 4:10).

The more one studies such utterances in their contexts, the more he sees the reason for the intense interest which the men of the New Testament take in the eternity and the immutability of the promise. They regard it as the charter of all the rights which they and their successors may possess as Christians. Further, they claim especially that the salvation of the gentiles through Christ comes under the promise. They make it emphatic that God's promise to Abraham was for the nations, and therefore conveys title to the gentiles, under which they may receive the gospel. Paul says to the Galatians:—"And the scripture, foreseeing that God would justify the Gentiles by faith, gave the gospel before unto Abraham, [saying], In thee shall all the nations be blessed" (3:8).[8]

Christ must be the ground of our hope; for only through Him can we be heirs to eternal life. An immortal inheritance is presented to us on certain conditions. We cannot inherit a possession in this world unless we have a title that is without a flaw, and our right to an inheritance in the world to come, must

---

8. Ibid., p. 188.

also be clearly proved through a faultless title. The line through which the heavenly inheritance is to come is plainly revealed in the Word of God. We must come under the provisions of the Abrahamic covenant, and the requirements are, "If ye be Christ's, then are ye Abraham's seed, and heirs according to the promise." If we are Christ's, our title to the heavenly inheritance is without a flaw, and in harmony with the provisions of the covenant of grace. Through grace we shall be able to make our calling and election sure, putting on the excellency of Christ in spirit and character. No one will be entitled to the heavenly inheritance who has not been purified, refined, ennobled, and sanctified.[9]

The promise first given to Adam, then renewed to Abraham is the foundation of the everlasting covenant which contains the promise of righteousness, everlasting life, and an inheritance in the earth made new to all who will believe like their "father" Abraham (Romans 4:13–16; James 2:21–23, etc.). All blessings, whether in the present life or for all eternity, are found in Christ our Righteousness, who is the earnest or guarantee of our inheritance (Ephesians 1:3–14).

Behold, the days come, saith the Lord, that I will raise unto David a righteous Branch, and a King shall reign and prosper, and shall execute judgment and justice in the earth. In His days Judah shall be saved, and Israel shall dwell safely: and this is His name whereby He shall be called, THE LORD OUR RIGHTEOUSNESS. (Jeremiah 23:5, 6; see also 33:14–16).

Our right to the promised inheritance comes only through the work of our Saviour. "The righteousness by which we are justified is imputed; the righteousness by which we are sanctified is imparted. The first is our title to heaven, the second is our fitness for heaven."[10]

---

9. Ellen G. White, "Christ the Ground of Our Hope," *The Messenger*, May, 10, 1893.

10. White, *Review and Herald*, June 4, 1895. "The proud heart strives to earn salvation; but both our title to heaven and our fitness for it are found in the righteousness of Christ. The Lord can do nothing toward the recovery of man until, convinced of his own weakness, and stripped of all self-sufficiency, he yields himself to the control of God. Then he can receive the gift that God is waiting to bestow. From the soul that feels his need, nothing is withheld. He has unrestricted access to Him in whom all fullness dwells." *Desire of Ages*, (Mountain View, Calif.: Pacific Press, 1940), p. 300.

21

Staking the Claim

Continuing with our discussion of the parallels between God's everlasting covenant and the royal land grant we find Genesis 13 bears resemblance to the surveying process of the grants. The grantee was instructed to "walk about in the land through its length and breadth," thus staking a literal claim on the land. Genesis 13:15 reflects the royal land grant element of perpetuity, and the building of an altar confirmed Abraham's faith that the land was a gift from God (Genesis 12:7, 8; 13:18).

The proclamation of the gift of land in Genesis 15 is also styled according to the prevalent judicial pattern. In the gift-deed of Abba-El to Yarimlim we read: "On that day Abba-El gave the city. ..." Similarly we read in Genesis 15:18: "On that day Yahweh concluded a covenant with Abraham saying: 'To your offspring I give this land.'" The phrase "on that day" in these instances certainly had legal implications. The delineation of the borders and the specification of the granted territories in vv. 18–21 indeed constitute an important part of the documents of grant in the ancient Near East.[1]

In the making of the *k-r-t berit*, "the principal party passes between the pieces. He is represented by the smoke and the fire, which are frequent symbols of the Divine Presence. As a legal document, the nature of the instrument of transfer is defined, its promissory clause is specified as concerning a grant of land, and the extent of the territory involved is delineated in geographic and ethnographic terms."[2]

---

1. Weinfeld, p. 82.
2. Sarna, *The JPS Torah Commentary on Genesis*, p. 117.

Once the terms of the covenant are specified, a validating ceremony takes place. "Chapter fifteen of Genesis constitutes the covenant ratification ceremony. In it the promises of the covenant are restated, the land is specifically described by the natural landmarks and by naming the adjacent lands, and an oath ceremony is conducted. There are parallels to the grant treaty in each of these."[3]

It should be noted that in this covenant ratification, the land has played a dominant role. While the covenant includes other blessings, such as a great name, innumerable progeny, protection and general blessing, in the ceremony itself, the land-grant has all but eclipsed these promises. The reason seems clear—the author intends to cast the covenant in the tradition of the land-grant.[4]

3. Hegg, p. 7.
4. Ibid., p. 10.

22

Land Grant Defines the Everlasting Kingdom of David

When David had obtained peace in his kingdom, was blessed with wealth and children, he desired to more fully serve the Lord who had given him all these blessings. His resident prophet was close at hand. One day David inquired of him, "See now, I dwell in a house of cedar, but the ark of God dwelleth within curtains." (2 Samuel 7:2). It seemed highly inappropriate for God's *Shechinah* glory to be "roughing it" in a tent rather than having a formally constructed place of rest. David thought it appropriate for him to use God's gifts to construct a permanent place for the ark of the covenant. However, God had other plans. David was not to be His architect and building contractor. Because David was a man of war, he was not allowed to build a sacred home for the ark of the covenant. That duty would fall on David's future son, who would be a man of peace.

Though David was disappointed in his building plans, he was not discouraged by the remainder of Nathan's prophecy. Through Nathan's prophecy, God renewed His land grant covenant with His beloved servant, a "man after [God's] own heart" (1 Samuel 13:14; Acts 13:22). When Nathan informed David of the details of his vision, he included a renewal of Jacob's prophecy that the "scepter shall not depart from Judah, nor a lawgiver from between his feet, until Shiloh come, and unto Him shall all the gathering of the people be" (Genesis 49:10).

Nathan said "and the Lord telleth me that He will make thee an house … and thine house and thy kingdom shall be established for ever before thee: thy throne shall be established for ever" (2 Samuel 7:11, 16). As with the promise given to Abraham, the term "house" includes the establishment of a family line that, as David's descendants for generations to come, would continue to inherit the land. Even after the nation of Israel was divided, right up until the Babylonian captivity, the southern section remained under the rule of one of David's offspring. Through Shiloh, the throne of David would be eternally established as the everlasting kingdom of God.[1]

Instead of arguing with Nathan or God regarding the issue, David simply agreed with God's plans. Like Abraham's "amen" (see Genesis 15:6), David's prayer is an acknowledgment of God's sovereignty and righteous judgment in all things (2 Samuel 7:18–29). David was called a man after God's own heart simply because his will was submitted, his heart was yielded, and his affections were fixed upon the promises of God—the covenant-keeping God. Such submission to the divine will foreshadowed that of David's coming Son who, as Servant of mankind, would empty Himself of all self-will and self-centered motivations, humbling Himself, making Himself of no reputation, and becoming obedient to the divine will for the salvation of the human race (John 5:30; Philippians 2:6–8). Such heart-felt devotion and allegiance toward God is the hallmark of true faith which results in righteousness.[2]

Since David was at peace in his realm, God only needed to renew His covenant promise. The covenant with Abraham was centered on land and seed (Genesis 12:1–3; and chapter 15); the renewal with David did the same (2 Samuel 7:11–16). God said: "I have made a covenant with My chosen, I have sworn unto David My servant, thy seed will I establish forever and build up thy throne to all generations." (Psalm 89:3, 4). The import of this sworn promise is the same as was given to Adam and Eve (Genesis 3:15), then to Abraham (Genesis 12:1–3; cf. Hebrews 6:16–18), that a "Seed" would come through whom all the earth would be blessed. Paul makes the same declaration that "to Abraham

---

1. Shiloh literally means "he whose it is" or "that which belongs to him" indicating that Shiloh is the rightful owner of the territory being granted to David and his descendants.

2. "There is danger in regarding justification by faith as placing merit on faith. When you take the righteousness of Christ as a free gift you are justified freely through the redemption of Christ. What is faith? The substance of things hoped for, the evidence of things not seen (Hebrews 11:1). It is an assent of the understanding to God's words which binds the heart in willing consecration and service to God, Who gave the understanding, Who moved on the heart, Who first drew the mind to view Christ on the cross of Calvary. Faith is rendering to God the intellectual powers, abandonment of the mind and will to God, and making Christ the only door to enter into the kingdom of heaven." Ellen G. White, *Faith and Works* (Nashville, Tenn.: Southern Publishing, 1979), p. 25.

and his seed were the promises made. He saith not, and to seeds, as of many; but as of one, and to thy Seed, which is Christ" (Galatians 3:16). For fulfillment, the promise required that a biological descendant of David would occupy his throne until Messiah came and inherited the kingdom. In an unbroken line, Jesus traced His genealogy back through his mother, not only to David, but on to Judah and Abraham and then to Adam (Luke 3:23–38).

Christ is the Last Adam, fully qualified to be the nearest of kin for the whole human race.[3] Thus we see that the everlasting covenant, which included the promise of land and the righteousness to possess it, was bound up with the promise of the coming Kinsman Redeemer who would ransom the lost possession from the control of Satan, the wily usurper who stole Adam's birthright from him. As King of kings, Jesus will set up a kingdom that will never be destroyed (Daniel 2:44).

---

3. "Of Christ's relation to His people, there is a beautiful illustration in the laws given to Israel. When through poverty a Hebrew had been forced to part with his patrimony, and to sell himself as a bondservant, the duty of redeeming him and his inheritance fell to the one who was nearest of kin. See Leviticus 25:25, 47-49; Ruth 2:20. So the work of redeeming us and our inheritance, lost through sin, fell upon Him who is 'near of kin' unto us. It was to redeem us that He became our kinsman. Closer than father, mother, brother, friend, or lover is the Lord our Saviour. 'Fear not,' He says, 'for I have redeemed thee, I have called thee by thy name; thou art Mine.' 'Since thou wast precious in My sight, thou hast been honorable, and I have loved thee: therefore will I give men for thee, and people for thy life.' Isaiah 43:1, 4." Ellen G. White, *Desire of Ages* (Mountain View, Calif.: Pacific Press, 1940), p. 327.

Part VI

Unilateral Gift from the King

23

Confirmation of the Covenant

While the events of Genesis 15:17 illustrate an affirmation or oath element of a land grant, it uses the method of a covenant of parity to underscore the uniqueness of the covenant now being signified by God in covenant promise to Abraham. In the ancient Near Eastern culture, a covenant of parity was a covenant of promise between equals to do or to refrain from doing something that was mutually beneficial to both of the promising parties. The parity covenant was usually sealed by the promising parties walking together between the halves of a sacrificial animal, such as a bullock or a ram. In essence, the parties were giving witness to each other that if either should break his promise, or fail to uphold his side of the covenant, then what had happened to the animal would fall also upon him.[1] This type of covenant had no connection to the suzerain covenant. The suzerain covenant was between a conqueror and his vassals, and involved specific stipulations which were binding on the weaker vassal nations. The suzerain covenant, by its very nature, was a covenant of unequalness.

Other instances of parity covenants in the Bible are found between Abraham and Abimelech in Genesis 21:22–32; and between Isaac and Abimelech in Genesis 26:26–31. In both cases the parties "made a covenant." The literal translation of the word "made" is "to cut," signifying that the covenants Abraham and Isaac formed with Abimelech were of a

---

1. "Covenants in which the two parties step between cloven animal parts are attested in various places in the ancient Near East, as well as in Greece. The idea is that if either party violates the covenant, his fate will be like that of the cloven animal. The Hebrew idiom *karat berit*, literally, to cut a covenant, may derive from this legal ritual." Robert Alter, *Genesis: A Translation and Commentary* (New York: W.W. Norton, 1996), p. 65.

type similar to the one we read about in Genesis chapter fifteen, being the common form of covenant in that culture.[2] In both of these cases it was a covenant of promise to refrain from war over the denial of certain property rights (e.g. the wells of water). Not all covenants of parity involved the cutting of a sacrifice, but this type of covenant was always made between two equal parties and was for the purpose of settling a dispute and creating a binding peace between the two parties. Other examples of covenants of parity are found in 1 Kings 5:1–12; 15:16–20; and 20:31–34. In the last reference we find Ahab not only gave his word, but he "cut" a covenant with Ben-hadad before sending him away in peace.

In Genesis 15, God restates the land grant covenant He made to Abraham when He called him out of Haran (Genesis 12:13), and now seals the promise with the ritual of the cutting of the pieces. Abraham did as he was instructed, cutting and laying out the slaughtered animals, evidently in anticipation of his participation in the covenant routine. "And it came to pass, that, when the sun went down, and it was dark, behold a smoking furnace, and a burning lamp that passed between those pieces" (Genesis 15:17). God purposely chose this parity form of covenant when sealing His land grant promise to Abraham. By doing so, God was saying to Abraham, "Let what happened to these animals happen to Me if I do not keep My promise to you to give you an inheritance of children and land." God was laying His eternal existence on the line in promising Abraham that He would give him an everlasting inheritance and the righteousness to obtain it. "In this covenant it is God who commits Himself and swears, as it were, to keep the promise. It is He accompanied by a smoking oven and blazing torch who passes between the parts as though He were invoking the curse upon Himself."[3]

In a covenant of parity it takes two to make the agreement. Variously, scholars have attempted to define what took place in this instance by (1) claiming that even though the Scripture does not specifically state that Abraham "walked" between the pieces, he must have done so because the covenant type demanded it; or (2) that God used this form of covenant intentionally but that only He passed between the pieces, making it a one-sided promise, with the curse falling only on Him. The

---

2. "To cut or carve; hence a covenant, from the custom of passing between the divided pieces of the victims slain on the occasion of making such solemn compacts." H.D. Spence and Joseph S. Exell, eds., *The Pulpit Commentary on Genesis* (Grand Rapids, Mich.: Eerdmans, 1962), p. 111.

3. Weinfeld, p. 79.

first explanation violates the everlasting covenant by making it a mutual affair between equals, an old covenant idea.[4] The second explanation is also a violation of the parity covenant formula because there could be no covenant without a witness of equal stature to attest to the binding aspects of the agreement.

Is there a reasonable explanation which satisfactorily defines what took place that evening in ancient Palestine?

Yes:—Reading the Scripture we see that there were two entities that passed between the animal parts, "a smoking furnace and a burning lamp."[5] The Godhead was present that evening on the hills between Bethel and Ai. The glorious theophany was a demonstration of the everlasting covenant between the Father and the Son that They would restore humanity's eternal inheritance should sin cause them to forfeit

---

4. "God promises us everything that we need, and more than we can ask or think, as a gift. We give Him ourselves, that is nothing. And He gives us Himself, that is everything. That which makes all the trouble is that even when men are willing to recognize the Lord at all they want to make bargains with Him. They want it to be an equal, mutual affair—a transaction in which they can consider themselves on a par with God. But whoever deals with God must deal with Him on His own terms, that is on a basis of fact—that we have nothing and are nothing, and He has everything and is everything and gives everything." E.J. Waggoner, *The Glad Tidings*, p. 71.

5. "That God should appear as fire is appropriate for many reasons. Just as all physical life depends on the fire that is the sun, so does all spiritual life depend on God. Just as fire both purifies and destroys, so does God purify the righteous and destroy the wicked. Just as fire lights up the blackness of night, so does God overcome the dark powers of evil. Just as fire is mysterious and immaterial so too is God enigmatic and incorporeal. And just as fire cannot be held for examination, so is God always the indefinable who is beyond our grasp." Leland Ryken, James C. Wilhoit and Tremper Longman, III, eds., *Dictionary of Biblical Imagery* (Downers Grove, Ill.: InterVarsity Press, 1998), p. 287.

Often in Scripture we find a dual manifestation of smoke and fire when the writer is speaking of God's presence among His people. "The coming of God's presence in the awesome fire and darkness of Mount Sinai appears to be intentionally reflected in Abraham's pyrotechnic vision." (John H. Sailhamer, *The Pentateuch as Narrative*, Grand Rapids, Mich.: Zondervan, 1992, p. 152).

Isaiah used the same representations for God when he wrote: "And the Lord will create upon every dwelling place of mount Zion, and upon her assemblies, a cloud and smoke by day, and the shining of a flaming fire by night: for upon all the glory shall be a defence." (Isaiah 4:5; see also Isaiah 31:9). Isaiah's reference is clearly to the manifestation of God during the wilderness wandering (Exodus 13:21-22).

it.[6] Both the Father and the Son passed between the pieces that evening giving visible evidence of the promise made from the foundation of the world (Genesis 3:15; Revelation 13:8; Titus 1:2; 1 Peter 1:19, 20). Present also as the eternal witness was the Holy Spirit who would testify of the truth of the everlasting covenant (John 15:26). The covenant of parity could not be made between God and Abraham, because no claim could be made that they were equals.[7] The covenant of parity could only be made between members of the Godhead who are eternally equal.

In the beginning was the Word, and the Word was with God, and the Word was God. The same was in the beginning with God (John 1:1, 2).

I and my Father are one (John 10:30).

Philip saith unto him, Lord, shew us the Father, and it sufficeth us. Jesus saith unto him, Have I been so long time with you, and yet hast thou not known me, Philip? he that hath seen me hath seen the Father; and how sayest thou then, Shew us the Father? (John 14:8, 9).

Thomas Brooks (1608-1680) declared in his treatise "Paradise Opened" that all members of the Godhead were present when the everlasting covenant was made.

---

6. "Jesus, knowing that all things were now accomplished, cried out with a loud voice, It is finished. The work that Thou gavest Me is accomplished. Thus He gave His dying testimony to men and angels that the work He came to earth to do was to save a perishing world by His death. When Christ spoke these words, He addressed His Father. Christ was not alone in making this great sacrifice. It was the fulfillment of the covenant made between the Father and the Son before the foundation of the earth was laid. With clasped hands they entered into the solemn pledge that Christ would become the substitute and surety for the human race if they were overcome by Satan's sophistry. The compact was now being fully consummated. The climax was reached. Christ had the consciousness that He had fulfilled to the letter the pledge He had made. In death He was more than conqueror. The redemption price has been paid. His right hand and His glorious holy arm have gotten Him the victory." (Ellen G. White, *Manuscript Releases* Vol. 12, p. 408; see also *Desire of Ages*, p. 834).

7 White, "Gospel Hearers," part 5, *Review and Herald*, June, 28, 1892: "It was to save the transgressor from ruin that He who was co-equal with God, offered up His life on Calvary."

Consent of all parties, the allowance of the judge, and public record, is as much as can be desired to make all public contracts authentic in courts of justice; and what can we desire more, to settle, satisfy, and assure our own souls that all the articles of the covenant of redemption shall, on all hands, be certainly made good, than this, that these three heavenly witness, God the Father, God the Son, and God the Holy Spirit, do all agree to the articles of the covenant, and are all witnesses to the same covenant?[8]

There was nothing greater by which God could swear except Himself. Paul helps us understand the covenant made with Abraham by describing the usual manner in which two men of equal stature swore to one another, "an oath for confirmation [which was] to them an end of all strife" (Hebrews 6:16; cf. Genesis 21:22–32). As we have previously detailed, through the making of the covenant of parity two men would sware to one another that all strife between them would be at an end. While there was no "strife" between the Father and the Son, there *was* a conflict between God and His creatures caused by Satan, which the Godhead assumed upon themselves to remedy.[9]

For when God made promise to Abraham, because He could swear by no greater, He sware by Himself, saying, surely blessing I will bless thee, and multiplying I will multiply thee. And so, after he had patiently endured, he obtained the promise. For men verily swear by the greater: and an oath for confirmation is to them an end of all strife. Wherein God, willing more abundantly to shew unto the heirs of promise the immutability of His counsel, confirmed it by an oath: that by two immutable things, in which it was impossible for God to lie, we might have a strong consolation, who have fled for refuge to lay hold upon the hope set before us (Hebrews 6:13–18).

---

8. Thomas Brooks, *The Works of Thomas Brooks* (Edinburgh: Banner of Truth, 1980 [1867]) 5:329-403; quoted in Ralph Allen Smith, *The Eternal Covenant* (Moscow, Ida.: Canon Press, 2003), pp. 19-20.

9. White, "Sin of Presumption," *Review and Herald*; April 1, 1875: "If Christ had been deceived by Satan's temptations, and had exercised His miraculous power to relieve Himself from difficulty, He would have broken the contract made with His Father, to be a probationer in behalf of the race." See also Zechariah 6:12-13.

God could find no one greater than Himself, so He made the oath "between" Himself.[10] Christ confirms that He and His Father are co-witnesses in the plan of salvation. "And yet if I judge, My judgment is true: for I am not alone, but I and the Father that sent Me. It is also written in your law, that the testimony of two men is true. I am one that bear witness of Myself, and the Father that sent Me beareth witness of Me" (John 8:16-18).

The "two immutable things" Paul mentions are first, the promise of God to give the land as an everlasting inheritance (and the righteousness required to receive the everlasting inheritance),[11] which in itself should have been sufficient for Abraham's enduring faith (Genesis 15:6). And secondly, the oath God made to Abraham in taking the curse upon Himself by "walking between the pieces," constituted a more abundant assurance of God's commitment to fulfill His promise. God's promise and His oath are both immutable, unchangeable, enduring forever, and unamendable.

Thus the royal land grant is seen in its uniqueness as the embodiment of the everlasting covenant; a fully legal and immutable promise to Abraham and his spiritual heirs. "There is neither Jew nor Greek, there is neither bond nor free, there is neither male nor female: for ye are all one in Christ Jesus. And if ye be Christ's, then are ye Abraham's seed, and heirs according to the promise" (Galatians 3:28, 29).

The everlasting covenant is the revelation of God's plan of redemption, enveloping the entire scope of God's redemptive promise to save lost humanity from their sin and restore to them their everlasting possession—this earth made new after sin and unrepentant sinners are destroyed in the lake of fire (Revelation 20:12–15; 21:1). "It is essential to note that the covenant is unilateral in its inception and the curses are given to protect Abraham, not to induce his loyalty or obedience." "The redemptive blessing to mankind is the ultimate promise and it is guaranteed as the gift of the King."[12]

---

10. White, *Manuscript Releases*, vol. 21, p. 195: "In the councils of heaven, before the world was created, the Father and the Son covenanted together that if man proved disloyal to God, Christ, one with the Father, would take the place of the transgressor, and suffer the penalty of justice that must fall upon him."

11. E.J. Waggoner, *The Glad Tidings*, p. 72.

12. Hegg, pp. 6 and 7.

24

It's All About Inheritance—by Faith in the Promise

W hen [Abraham's] father was dead, He removed him into this land, wherein ye now dwell. And He gave him none inheritance in it, no, not so much as to set his foot on: yet He promised that He would give it to him for a possession, and to his seed after him, when as yet he had no child" (Acts 7:5).

How could God say Abraham had inherited the land when this verse clearly states he never actually owned even the ground impressed by his sandals? Why did God call Abraham to leave his homeland in Ur and travel to a foreign country? (Genesis 12:1). Why did God tell Abraham He was going to give him every part of the land of Canaan, everywhere he put his foot (Genesis 13:17) would be his, when in fact Abraham never owned anything in Canaan except a grave, and that he purchased for himself? (see Genesis 23:3–16).

The issue of inheritance was not about the physical dirt and bushes of Palestine. The covenant with Abraham encompassed much more than earthly physical territory. After describing Abraham and Sarah's experience in conceiving the miracle child, Paul declares:—

These all died in faith, not having received the promises, but having seen them afar off, and were persuaded of them, and embraced them, and confessed that they were strangers and pilgrims on the earth. For they that say such things declare plainly that they seek a country. And truly, if they had been mindful of that country from whence they came out, they might have had opportunity to have returned. But now they desire a better country, that is, an heavenly: wherefore God is not ashamed to be called their God: for He hath prepared for them a city … and these all, having obtained a good report through faith, received not the promise: God having provided some better thing for us, that they without us should not be made perfect (Hebrews 11:13–16, 39, 40).

The word inherit occurs sixty-two times in the Bible, thirteen times in the New Testament, all in the context of inheriting the promise of the new earth and eternal life to enjoy it. The words heir or heirs in a combined count occur twenty-eight times, most in the New Testament in the context of the Gospel. The word inheritance occurs 239 times in the Bible, the vast majority being concentrated in the books of Numbers, Deuteronomy, Joshua, and the Psalms, where the discussion revolves around the literal occupation of the land of Canaan, or Palestine. Because of the promise God made to their father Abraham it cannot be denied that the children of Israel did inherit the literal dirt and bushes of the land of Canaan. However, the inheritance was not given to the children of Israel because of anything they had done to deserve it. Moses makes this very clear:—

> Not for thy righteousness, or for the uprightness of thine heart, dost thou go to possess their land: but for the wickedness of these nations the LORD thy God doth drive them out from before thee, and that He may perform the word which the LORD sware unto thy fathers, Abraham, Isaac, and Jacob. Understand therefore, that the LORD thy God giveth thee not this good land to possess it for thy righteousness; for thou art a stiffnecked people (Deuteronomy 9:5, 6).

Included in the promise of the inheritance of the land was the promise of rest—spiritual rest. When the Lord was grieved by the continued, irrational unbelief of His people, He finally adjudged them unfit to inherit His promise (Numbers 14:11, 12). In behalf of the children of Israel, but also in defence of God's character and claiming the promise of God's longsuffering mercy toward sinners (vv. 13–19), Moses intervened to save the people from imminent destruction. The adults of the group were condemned to die in the desert without ever seeing the land for which they longed, but those under 20 years of age were still eligible to inherit the promise given to their fathers Abraham, Isaac, and Jacob.

Even though they did enter into the physical land of Canaan, the apostle Paul tells us they never succeeded in gaining the promise of spiritual rest for the same reason—continued unbelief. "So we see that they could not enter in [to His rest] because of unbelief" (Hebrews 3:19).

Paul reminded the Jewish people of his day that, as a whole, they had never accepted the everlasting covenant given to Abraham (Hebrews chapters 3 and 4). They remain outside the everlasting rest God intended to bestow upon them if they would be faithful and loyal to His promises to their father Abraham. Paul makes it clear that he is discussing spiritual rest when he ties God's spiritual rest to the seventh-day Sabbath (Hebrews 4:4–8), which is the sign and seal of the everlasting covenant.

God gave the Sabbath to His people to be a continual sign of His love and mercy and of their obedience. As He rested on this day and was refreshed, so He desired His people to rest and be refreshed. It was to be a constant reminder to them that they were included in His covenant of grace. Throughout your generations, He said, the Sabbath is to be My sign, My pledge, to you that I am the Lord that doth sanctify you, that I have chosen you and set you apart as My peculiar people. And as you keep the Sabbath holy, you will bear testimony to the nations of the earth that you are My chosen people.[1]

Spiritual rest can only be obtained though faith in God's finished work. "For we which have believed do enter into rest, as He said, As I have sworn in My wrath, if they shall enter into My rest: although the works were finished from the foundation of the world. ... For he that is entered into His rest, he also hath ceased from his own works, as God did from His" (Hebrews 4:2, 10). Throughout ancient Israel's history trampling of the Sabbath remained an issue and an outward sign of their continual unbelief (see Nehemiah 15:13–22; Isaiah 56:2–7; Jeremiah 17:21–27; Ezekiel 22:8; 23:38; and Amos 8:5).

Because of the legalism adopted after their Babylonian captivity, Israel attempted to build a hedge around the Sabbath formulating thirty-nine "father laws" which, by the time of Christ, added an accumulation of more than 600 man-made proscriptions concerning Sabbath-keeping. In part, it was against these obscuring encumbrances that Jesus proclaimed His condemnation of the Pharisees: "For they bind heavy burdens and grievous to be borne, and lay them on men's shoulders" (Matthew 23:4). The Sabbath had lost its true meaning as a sign of faith, confidence and rest in God's finished work of salvation.

Paul declared plainly that the necessary righteousness to obtain the inheritance does not come through the law or though law-keeping,

---

1. Ellen G. White, *Review and Herald*, October 28, 1902.

but only by faith in the promise of God through Christ and His righteousness. "For if the inheritance be of the law, it is no more of promise: but God gave it to Abraham by promise." "For if they which are of the law be heirs, faith is made void, and the promise made of none effect" (Galatians 3:18; Romans 4:14; see also Galatians 4:22–26).

We may significantly note that unlike the land grant, there were no provisions in the suzerain covenant for an inheritance of any kind. All the vassal could receive under the suzerain covenant was perpetual bondage to the suzerain. In contradistinction, the Gospel is all about inheriting—spiritual rest, eternal life, and the earth made new. For the everlasting covenant, we must look to a covenant that includes an inheritance. The only place we find this promise is in the covenant God made with Abraham. Sinai is devoid of any such provision.

25

Circumcision—an Amendment to the Everlasting Covenant?

We have examined the royal land grant formula as it seems to follow the pattern set forth in the everlasting covenant which was in place from before the foundation of the world. Because some see the rite of circumcision as an addition to the everlasting covenant, we must now address the next chapters in the Genesis narrative. Does Genesis chapter 17 add stipulations to the unilateral covenant given to Abraham in chapters 12 through 15? Does the "amendment" of the rite of circumcision change the everlasting covenant from an unconditional covenant into a conditional one? Does God add covenant stipulations and curses to an otherwise unilateral promise? What does God mean when He tells Abraham: "And the uncircumcised man child whose flesh of his foreskin is not circumcised, that soul shall be cut off from his people; he hath broken My covenant" (Genesis 17:14)?

We must also examine the message in chapter 17 within the literary structure of the entire narrative of Genesis chapters 12–25, which is divided into two sections: chapters 12–17 and chapters 18–25. The obvious change of scene in chapter 18 marks the end of one subsection and beginning of another, while chapter 17 functions as the pivotal text bringing in a summary of the previous five chapters (vss. 1–8) and advancing the reader to the realities of the promise in the chapters that follow (vss. 15–19). The focal element in chapter 17 is the rite of circumcision, but within the immediate context of the previously given everlasting covenant.

Some insist the rite of circumcision was an amendment to the everlasting covenant given in Genesis 15, and therefore changes the original covenant into a suzerain treaty which includes curses as well as blessings.

Arguing that the Abrahamic covenant follows the pattern of a suzerain treaty, and is therefore conditional, Kline interprets circumcision as a covenant ritual depicting self-malediction in connection with the covenant curses. ... Most agree that the Mosaic legislation as found in Exodus and Deuteronomy follows the pattern of the suzerain treaty. Kline, however, is in the minority when he states that the Abrahamic Covenant follows this same pattern or structure.[1]

Does circumcision constitute an amendment to the everlasting covenant transforming what appears to be a unilateral promise on the part of God into a suzerain contract requiring the performance of certain stipulations on the part of the recipient of the promise? Why was circumcision given to Abraham?

The key to our understanding the riddle of circumcision is contained in the previous chapter. After the everlasting covenant was signified in a most awesome manner, God declared the boundaries of the land grant by naming specific geological and clan identifiers, thus symbolically putting the "kudurru stones" in place. The next verse restates a known fact by emphatically declaring that Abram's wife, Sarai, was infertile, incapable of conception of the promised child. The reader is compelled to ask the same question Abraham asked in Genesis 15:2, 3: What good does the promise of land do for Abraham if he has no heirs to inherit it after he's gone? How can the gift be considered "perpetual" without a child who would inherit after Abraham's death?

Sarai produces an obvious human solution to the dilemma—a surrogate mother through the servant girl Hagar. "And Abram hearkened to the voice of Sarai" (Genesis 16:2). Condensed in rapid succession in the narrative is Abraham's apparent willingness to accept this commonly condoned method for handling the barrenness of a wife,[2] Hagar's conception; Sarai's anger over the slave's arrogant attitude of superiority toward her mistress as a result of her ability to conceive Abraham's child; the imminent birth of the child; Hagar's expulsion

---

1. Tim Hegg, "The Theological Significance of Circumcision," p. 4; article retrieved from the Internet on October 4, 2003 from: http://www.torahresource.com/cirucmcision.pdf

2. There are numerous parallels to the Biblical narrative and ancient Near Eastern documents showing the use of surrogates to obtain children. For example see, K. Grayson and J. Van Seters, "The Childless Wife in Assyria and the Stories of Genesis," *Orientalia*, vol. 44 (1975), pp. 485-486; and the *Anchor Bible Commentary* on Genesis.

from the family; God's intervention; and Ishmael's birth. At least nine months are contracted into the space of sixteen verses.

In these sixteen verses we see the outworking of man's attempt to fulfill the covenant promise of God. Instead of believing the word of the LORD, Abraham chose to listen to the words of his wife. "They reasoned that God had promised them a large family, but that since it was impossible for her to have children it was very evident He intended that they should use some other means of bringing it about. Thus it is that human reason deals with the promises of God."[3] Human reasoning without faith resulted in disaster: violation of God's "oneness" principle for marriage (Genesis 2:24); the needless contention between Abraham and his wife Sarai; conflict between Sarai and her servant; the manifestation of pride in Hagar; the near death of Hagar and her unborn child; and the birth of a child that would be the source of constant struggle and distress until the end of time.

Throughout the Abrahamic narrative God proved that He is more than able to deliver on His promise. Abraham's lack of faith which resulted in his taking Hagar as a concubine, necessitated the institution of the rite of circumcision.

> Human enterprise and strength would not be the means by which God would fulfill His promise to Abraham regarding the seed. Circumcision, the cutting away of the foreskin, revealed this explicitly. Coming on the heels of God's renewed promise to Abraham regarding his progeny and his installation as a father of a multitude of nations [Genesis 17:4–8], the sign of circumcision upon the organ of procreation must be interpreted within the narrative flow as relating to the method by which the complication (absence of children and age of both Abraham and Sarah) would be resolved. The promise would come, not by the strength of the flesh (which the "Hagar plan" represented) but rather by above-human means.[4]

Circumcision of the flesh was symbolic of the true circumcision of the heart, which is righteousness by faith. "Circumcision of the heart is that condition of the heart by which we will 'love the LORD' our God, 'with all the heart and with all the soul.' Then you see that that which this

---

3. Ellet J. Waggoner, *The Everlasting Covenant* (Berrien Springs, Mich.: Glad Tidings Publishers, 2002), p. 60.

4. Hegg, p. 16.

circumcision in the flesh was to Abraham, was simply a sign, a token, that they could see in the time when God was teaching them by object lessons—a token which they could see, signifying that which they could not see." [5]

For he is not a Jew, which is one outwardly; neither is that circumcision, which is outward in the flesh: but he is a Jew, which is one inwardly; and circumcision is that of the heart, in the spirit, and not in the letter; whose praise is not of men, but of God (Romans 2:28, 29).

And the father of circumcision to them who are not of the circumcision only, but who also walk in the steps of that faith of our father Abraham, which he had being yet uncircumcised. For the promise, that he should be the heir of the world, was not to Abraham, or to his seed, through the law, but through the righteousness of faith. For if they which are of the law be heirs, faith is made void, and the promise made of none effect: because the law worketh wrath: for where no law is, there is no transgression. Therefore it is of faith, that it might be by grace; to the end the promise might be sure to all the seed; not to that only which is of the law, but to that also which is of the faith of Abraham; who is the father of us all (Romans 4:12–16).

And if ye be Christ's, then are ye Abraham's seed, and heirs according to the promise (Galatians 3:29).

And ye are complete in Him, which is the head of all principality and power: in whom also ye are circumcised with the circumcision made without hands, in putting off the body of the sins of the flesh by the circumcision of Christ (Colossians 2:11).

Why did Christ become a curse on the tree? That the blessing of Abraham might come on you and me. Why did He redeem us from the curse of the law? That the blessing of Abraham might come on you and me. What is the blessing of Abraham? [Congregation: "Righteousness by faith."] Christ died that you and I might be made righteous by faith. Brethren, isn't it awful when a man will rob Christ of the very thing for which He died, and want righteousness in some other way? Isn't it awful? Brethren, let us believe in Jesus Christ. ... Then, when

---

5. A.T. Jones, *1893 General Conference Bulletin*, p. 399.

we as a people, we as a body, we as a church, have received the blessing of Abraham, what then? [Congregation: "The latter rain."] The outpouring of the Spirit. It is so with the individual. When the individual believes in Jesus Christ, and obtains the righteousness which is by faith, then the Holy Spirit, which is the circumcision of the heart, is received by him. And when the whole people, as a church, receive the righteousness of faith, the blessing of Abraham, then what is to hinder the church from receiving the Spirit of God? [Congregation: "Nothing."] That is where we are. What is to hinder, then, the outpouring of the Holy Spirit? What holds back the outpouring of the Holy Ghost? [Voice: "Unbelief."] [6]

In Genesis 15:6 Abraham was "accounted righteous" by his faith in God's promise to him that he would have children as innumerable as the stars of the heavens.

> Since faith is the depending upon the word of God only, for what that word says, being justified by faith is simply being accounted righteous by depending upon the word only. And since the word is the word of God, dependence upon the word only is dependence upon God only, in the word. Justification by faith, then, is justification—being accounted righteous by dependence upon God only; and upon him only because he has promised.[7]

Even though he previously had been given every evidence that God was more than capable of producing that which He had promised, Abraham's faith wavered as he attempted to fulfill God's promise through his own power. Circumcision showed the utter futility of depending upon the flesh for the fulfillment of God's promises. It added nothing to the covenant God had previously made with Abraham. "For we say that faith was reckoned to Abraham for righteousness. How was it then reckoned? when he was in circumcision, or in uncircumcision? Not in circumcision, but in uncircumcision. And he received the sign of circumcision, a seal of the righteousness of the faith which he had yet being uncircumcised" (Romans 4:9–11).

---

6. Jones, p. 383.

7. A.T. Jones, "Lessons on Faith," article in *Review and Herald*, February 14, 1899, republished in *Lessons on Faith* (Angwin, Calf.: Pacific Union College Press, 1987), p. 33.

Appropriately, circumcision of the organ of procreation was used by God to demonstrate to Abraham that the promised seed could not come through ordinary human effort, but only through divine intervention.

> The promises of the covenant come by Divine action directed in grace toward Abraham. He must receive the promise on the basis of faith (15:6) without relying upon the flesh. This is the heart of the covenant and it is to this that circumcision points. Circumcision is an outward sign to Abraham and to his progeny that the promised seed in whom 'all the nations of the earth would be blessed' would not come by human effort (as did Ishmael) but rather by the miraculous power of the Divine. In this way circumcision marked the necessity of faith as the promise of the seed was anticipated by each subsequent generation.[8]

For all subsequent generations who would follow, the sign of circumcision would remind them that salvation cannot come through human effort, but only by divine intervention in the human predicament and by our uncompromising faith in that divine promise and God's supernatural work.

---

8. Hegg, p. 18.

Part VII

Suzerain Treaty Contrasted with Royal Land Grant

26

Hebrew Distinction Between Covenants

When compared to the suzerain treaty covenant, land grants have a different focus, function, and purpose. "While the 'treaty' constitutes an obligation of the vassal to his master, the suzerain, the 'grant' constitutes an obligation of the master to his servant. In the 'grant' the curse is directed toward the one who will violate the rights of the king's vassal, while in the treaty the curse is directed toward the vassal who will violate the rights of the king. In other words, the 'grant' serves mainly to protect the rights of the servant while the treaty protects the rights of the master. What is more, while the grant is a reward for loyalty and good deeds already performed, the treaty is an inducement for future loyalty."[1]

Since the mid-1940s, a debate has developed among Old Testament evangelical scholars as to the exact meaning of the word *berit* (Hebrew for covenant). Some, following the form-critical approach, have contended that Wellhausen's view was correct, which claims *berit* was not used until late in the history of Israel. "Perlitt reverted to the old Wellhausen view that all references to *berit* in the old Testament are late—no earlier than the Deuteronomic materials. Every mention of a *berit* in the Sinai accounts is eliminated by literary-critical procedures. For Perlitt, the account of Yahweh's *berit* with Abraham in Genesis 15 in its present form was an early Deuteronomic document to be dated at the beginning of the seventh century." After a thorough study of the word *berit*, Ernst Kutsch concluded the primary meaning of the word was "obligation." "It never means a relationship, an alliance, or a covenant, but always an obligation."[2]

---

1. Weinfeld, pp. 69-70.

2. Ralph L. Smith, *Old Testament Theology* (Nashville, Tenn.: Broadman & Holman, 1993), p. 147.

However, other theologians took a completely opposite view of the meaning of the covenant. In 1944, Joachim Begrich published an article on the covenants in which he argued that "*berit* referred to a relationship between two unequal partners whereby the stronger gave to the weaker the assurance of friendly behavior and protection. Only the stronger was bound by the covenant. The weaker remained completely passive. Begrich believed God's covenant with Israel was originally a covenant of promise and assurance. Only after Israel settled in Canaan and adopted Canaanite conception of law was the donor *berit* changed into a contractual *berit* with obligations on both sides."[3]

Alfred Jepsen agreed with Begrich that "*berit* carried the idea of assurance from the stronger to the weaker party. Jepsen insisted that the covenant between God and Israel was never understood in legal or contractual terms, no obligation was ever imposed on Israel except that of renouncing the worship of other gods. This was a 'moral obligation,' not a law."[4]

Though the word "covenant" (*berit*) is used in both the Abrahamic and the Sinaitic narratives, there is in the original Hebrew a distinct difference between the term when used for a grant and the term when used in the context of a treaty. "The grant and the treaty alike were named *berit*, a word which conveys the general idea of an obligation concerning two parties ..." However, "as we have already seen, the deuteronomic sources refer to the Abrahamic and Davidic covenants as *habberit wehahesed* ('the gracious covenant') in contradistinction to the covenants of Sinai and the Plains of Moab which are referred to as *berit* only."[5]

Though sometimes equated with the suzerain covenant formula, the royal land grant contains some distinct differences which clearly distinguish it from the suzerain covenant. These differences include the fact that the suzerain covenant was written for the protection and rights of the suzerain and these are the only things guaranteed by the treaty. In the suzerain treaty, it is the vassal who makes the oath of obedience to the stipulations of the treaty (from the lesser individual to the greater). The suzerain treaty invariably contained curses against the vassal for violation of the contract stipulations—disobedience or rebellion against the suzerain. "The primary purpose of the suzerainty treaty

---

3. Ibid., p. 146.
4. Ibid., p. 147.
5. Weinfeld, p. 73.

was to establish a firm relationship between the suzerain and his vassal, including military support from the suzerain. However, the interests of the suzerain were primary. Its form was unilateral. The stipulations were binding only on the vassal, although a prologue often related the suzerain's benevolent deeds in behalf of the vassal."[6]

Contrary to these points of the suzerain covenant, the royal land grant covenant was written for the sole benefit of the recipient of the promise. The only curses contained in the land grant were against any individual who would dare to infringe upon the rights of the recipient of the land, and upon the grantor if he should fail to provide to the grantee what he had promised. Interestingly, the royal land grant covenant didn't necessarily include an oath, but if there was an oath included it was made by the king giving the land to the favored individual (from the greater individual to the lesser) and followed something along the lines of "May I be cursed if I take back what I gave you."[7]

This is the point upon which Moses later chided with God:—

> Remember Thy servants, Abraham, Isaac, and Jacob; look not unto the stubbornness of this people, nor to their wickedness, nor to their sin: lest the land whence thou broughtest us out say, because the LORD was not able to bring them into the land which He promised them, and because He hated them, He hath brought them out to slay them in the wilderness. Yet they are Thy people and Thine inheritance, which Thou broughtest out by Thy mighty power and by Thy stretched out arm (Deuteronomy 9:27–29).

6. Smith, p. 141.

7. Hegg, p. 3.

Compare and Contrast the Two Covenant Formulas

In summary of these discussions on the two covenant formulas, we are providing a chart which contains the elements of both the suzerain and the royal land grant covenants.

Suzerain Contract	Royal Land Grant Covenant
1. Were instituted to protect the suzerain from rebellion and disloyalty on the part of his vassals	1. Were instituted for the benefit of the grantee (recipient)
2. Preamble	2. Unilateral gift and bestowal of real property for the vassal's faithful and loyal service to the king
3. Historical prologue	
4. Stipulations	3. Preamble that identifies the grantor
5. Provision for deposition and periodic reading of the covenant	4. Historical reason for the grant
6. List of witnesses (gods who would carry out the curses)	5. Grantee's rights were guaranteed, defended and protected by the king
7. Blessings and curses	6. Royal land grants were considered perpetual, inheritable, and "forever"
8. A formal oath on the part of the vassal	7. If an oath was made during the ratification ceremony, only the king made the oath, which included the promise of protection to his vassal
9. Solemn ceremony	
10. Formulation for initiating action against the rebellious vassal (guidelines for a covenant lawsuit)	8. Land grants contained blessings for the grantee, but curses for anyone who would violate the grantee's rights

Part VIII

The Historic Position

21

Covenant Theology in America

We must remember that nothing happens in a vacuum; all things are related to and influenced by what had preceded it historically. An assessment of the early Adventist understanding of the covenants can only be appreciated by examining the theological environment that produced it.

When America was first colonized by the Puritans, "covenant theology" was barely a century old. For the first two hundred years of this country's settlement, covenant theology among the New England churches was decidedly Calvinistic, following the Reformed federalist covenant theology developed during the Protestant Reformation. Prior to the Reformation, covenant theology was present in the teaching of the church, but lay quiescent and undeveloped.

Augustine of Hippo (b. 354, d. 430) laid the cornerstone for the Reformation covenant discussion with his work, *The City of God*, which stated that there are two covenants—a covenant of works and a covenant of grace. Augustine believed that God had placed Adam under a legal covenant of works by placing him under law and demanding obedience. The tree of life was the sign of this primal covenant. From Augustine's idea sprang the major theological position of the medieval church: God can only call people righteous if they truly are righteous inside and out.

However, according to the church such righteousness could only occur through the infusion of divine grace through the sacraments administered by the priests. Justification was therefore a matter of the individual's cooperation with divine grace; faith and obedience were viewed as equivalent terms.

In practical terminology, this meant that man was justified by his works of obedience. A slight spin on this was the more lax position of

William of Ockham (1285-1347) and Gabriel Biel (1420-1495), who formulated the proposition that God rewards sinners with a kind of merit for effort. If the individual exerts an effort to obey, then God overlooks his sins and treats him as though he had fulfilled the terms of the covenant. "God helps those who help themselves" is the a proverbial saying that grew from this theological position.

In reaction to these covenantal propositions Martin Luther (1483-1546), John Calvin (1509-1564), and other Protestant theologians rejected the idea of human merit obtained through church sacraments or personal works. Luther and Calvin both claimed that salvation was by faith alone in the merits of Christ. Curiously and seemingly contrary to this position, both men held the double predestination theory of absolute divine sovereignty over salvation—the individual has no free will and no influence in the final outcome of God's judgment of humanity. "Election" is predetermined by the sovereignty of God who, from eternity past, has preordained who will be saved and who will be eternally dammed.

Luther attempted to resolve his dilemma by distinguishing between the covenant of Law and the covenant of Grace. In his later writings, Luther dropped his discussion of covenant theology, leaving the development of this thorny topic for men like Calvin, Huldrych Zwingli (1484-1531) and John Oecolampadius (1482-1531).

Oecolampadius developed what would come to be expressed as the Reformed theological position on the covenants. He taught that the Father *required* that the Son should function in the place of the Elect, obeying *instead of them* (the "elect" have no need to obey, Christ obeyed *for* them), and atoning vicariously[1] for their sins by meeting the demands of the original covenant of works which Adam had failed to accomplish. Under this agreement between the Father and the Son, the Father promised several things, one of which was that the Son would be given a sinless human nature through which to work out His obedience as the last Adam.

Oecolampadius' most important contribution to the covenant discussion was in the area of the covenant of grace. He claimed that the covenant of grace was one-sided in origin and two-sided in

---

1. Vicarious means to experience or realize through imaginative or sympathetic participation in the experience of another without having any actual participation in the event or action. Vicarious atonement means that Christ's death in actuality had nothing to do with us personally, but was completely external to our experience in meeting the just demands of the broken law of God.

administration. God's *offer* of grace was unconditional from the viewpoint that mankind could not anticipate nor prepare for it. However, as a response to this offer of grace Christians are obligated to attend to preaching and the sacraments.

Coupled with Calvin's classic federal position which stated that there were three covenants: (1) the covenant of redemption in eternity, (2) the covenant of works before the Fall, and (3) the covenant of grace after the Fall, Oecolampadius' position was the basic Reformed theological view on the covenants through the nineteenth century.

From this puissant seedbed sprang the Puritan movement which entailed a blending of spiritualism and legalism in its efforts to control the morality of its adherents.[2] Puritan colonists in New England brought with them their covenant ideas, ideas forged in the Protestant Reformation and the theologically stormy years following the Counsel of Trent.

Building upon a false premise, a logical argument may be constructed, but logic does not create truth no matter how well constructed the argument appears.

---

2. Information summarized from Ralph A. Smith: *Eternal Covenant* (Moscow, Ida.: Canon Press, 2003) and an article written by R. Scott Clark: "A Brief History of Covenant Theology," published on the Internet by Westminister Seminary, California; document retrieved January 25, 2004 from: http://public.csusm.edu/public/guests/rsclark/history_covenant

28

E.J. Waggoner's View of the Everlasting Covenant

The following section contains direct statements reproduced in context from E.J. Waggoner's writings. This was done to allow Waggoner to be clearly understood regarding his exposition of God's everlasting covenant. References for the various sources appear at the end of each subsection.

While Waggoner never used the legal term "land grant," his exposition from Scripture does use language fitting the definition of a land grant covenant. It will be seen that Waggoner unceasingly referred to the covenant God made with Abraham as the "everlasting covenant," and that this covenant included an inheritance of land—the whole earth made new—*and* the necessary righteousness with which to obtain it. The concept of land, freely and legally given, is embedded as an integral component of the ancient royal land grant, as we have shown in this study. Waggoner's teaching on the everlasting covenant parallels the royal land grant covenant.

Good News from the Book of Galatians

Below we quote him in full.

That the thing promised, and the sum of all the promises, is an inheritance is clearly seen from Galatians 3:15–18. The sixteenth verse tells us that the law, coming in four hundred and thirty years after the promise was made and confirmed, cannot make that promise of none effect. "For if the inheritance is by the law, it is no longer by promise; but God gave it to Abraham by a promise" (verse 18). What this promised inheritance is may be seen by comparing the verse just quoted with Romans 4:13: The promise to Abraham and his descendants, that they should inherit the world, did not come through the law but through the righteousness of faith. And so, although the heavens and earth which are now "reserved unto fire against the day of judgment and perdition of ungodly men," when "the heavens being on fire shall be dissolved, and the elements shall melt with fervent heat," "we, according to His promise, look for new heavens and a new earth, wherein dwelleth righteousness" (2 Peter 3:7, 12, 13). This is the heavenly country for which Abraham, Isaac, and Jacob looked.

"Christ redeemed us from the curse … that we might receive the promise of the Spirit through faith." This "promise of the Spirit" we have seen to be the possession of the whole earth made new—redeemed from the curse. For "the creation itself will be set free from its bondage to decay and obtain the glorious liberty of the children of God" (Romans 8:21). The earth fresh and new from the hand of God, perfect in every respect, was given to man for a possession (Genesis 1:27, 28, 31). Man sinned and brought the curse upon himself. Christ has taken the whole curse, both of man and of all creation, upon Himself. He redeems the earth from the curse, that it may be the everlasting possession that God originally designed it to be; and He also redeems man from the curse, that he may be fitted for the possession of such an inheritance. This is the sum of the gospel. "The free gift of God is eternal life in Jesus Christ our Lord" (Romans 6:23). This gift of eternal life is included in the promise of the inheritance, for God promised the land to Abraham and to his seed for "an everlasting possession" (Genesis 17:8). It is an inheritance of righteousness, because the promise that Abraham should be heir of the world was through the righteousness of faith. Righteousness, eternal life, and a place in which to live eternally—these are all in the promise, and they are all that could possibly be desired or given. To redeem man, but to give him no place in which to live, would be an incomplete work. The two actions are parts of one whole. The power by which we are redeemed is the power of creation, by which the heavens and the earth are made new. When all is accomplished, "there shall be no more curse" (Revelation 22:3).

The covenant and promise of God are one and the same. This is clearly seen from Galatians 3:17, where Paul asserts that to disannul the covenant would be to make void the promise. In Genesis 17 we read that God made a covenant with Abraham to give him the land of Canaan for an everlasting possession. Galatians 3:18 says that God gave it to him by promise. God's covenants with men can be nothing else than promises to them: "Who hath first given to Him, and it shall be recompensed unto him again? For of Him, and through Him, and to Him, are all things" (Romans 11:35, 36).[1]

Romans Record of Inheritance by Faith

A very natural inquiry upon reading the thirteenth verse [of Romans 4] would be, Where is there any promise that Abraham and his seed should be heirs of the world? Many think that no such promise is contained in the Old Testament. But there can be no doubt about the matter, for the apostle says that there was such a promise. If we have not found it, it is because we have read the Old Testament too superficially, or with minds biased by preconceived opinions. If we consider the connection, we shall have no difficulty in locating the promise.

Of what is the apostle speaking in this connection? Of an inheritance through the righteousness of faith, and also of the fact that circumcision was given to Abraham as a seal of this righteousness which he had by faith, and therefore as the seal of the inheritance which was to come thereby.

Where in the Old Testament do we find the account of the giving of circumcision, and of a promise in connection therewith? In the seventeenth chapter of Genesis. Then that must be the place for us to look for the promise that Abraham should be the heir of the world. Let us turn and read:—

> And I will establish My covenant between Me and thee and thy seed after thee in their generations, for an everlasting covenant, to be a God unto thee and to thy seed after thee. And I will give unto thee, and to thy seed after thee, the land wherein thou art a stranger, all the land of Canaan, for an everlasting possession; and I will be their God. ... And ye shall circumcise the flesh of your foreskin; and it shall be a token of the covenant betwixt Me and you (Genesis 17:7–11).

The reader will at once say: "Yes; it is plain enough that there is a promise here; but what we are looking for is the promise that Abraham and his seed should inherit the earth; and I do not see that here. All that I can see is a promise that they should inherit the land of Canaan."

But it is certain from the connection in Romans that we are on the right track, and we shall soon see that this is indeed the promise that Abraham and his seed should be heirs of the world. We must study the details of this promise. And first let us note the fact that the inheritance

---

1. Waggoner, *The Glad Tidings*, pp. 70-71.

promised is an everlasting inheritance. [Not a temporal or earthly one as some suppose the land of Palestine to be.]

Abraham himself is to have it for an everlasting possession. But the only way in which both Abraham and his seed may have everlasting possession of an inheritance is by having everlasting life. Therefore we see that in this promise to Abraham we have the assurance of everlasting life in which to enjoy the possession.

This will appear still more clearly when we consider that the inheritance is an inheritance of righteousness: "For the promise, that he should be the heir of the world, was not to Abraham, or to his seed, through the law, but through the righteousness of faith." Romans 4:13. That is just what we have in the promise recorded in the seventeenth of Genesis. For that covenant was sealed by circumcision (see verse 11), and circumcision was the seal of righteousness by faith. See Romans 4:11.

Someone may say that this does not appear from the Old Testament itself, and that therefore the Jews could not be expected to have understood it; we have the New Testament to enlighten us. It is true that in studying the Old Testament we owe much to the New Testament, but it is also a fact that there is no new revelation in it. One may see from the Old Testament alone that the inheritance promised to Abraham and to his seed was only on the condition of righteousness by faith.

This is the natural conclusion from the fact that the inheritance is to be an everlasting possession. Now the Jews well knew that everlasting life belongs to the righteous alone. "The righteous shall never be removed; but the wicked shall not inhabit the earth" (Proverbs 10:30). "For evildoers shall be cut off; but those that wait upon the Lord, they shall inherit the earth" (Psalm 37:9). "For such as be blessed of Him shall inherit the earth; and they that be cursed of Him shall be cut off" (vs. 22).

The fifth commandment reads, "Honor thy father and thy mother; that thy days may be long upon the land which the Lord thy God giveth thee." The keeping of the commandments has never made any difference in the length of men's lives in this present world. But the inheritance which God promised to Abraham is one that will be everlasting because of the righteousness of its possessors.

Another point from the promise is recorded in Genesis, if we read carefully. The promise was to Abraham and to his seed. Now Stephen stated as a well-known fact that Abraham did not have so much of the promised land as he could set his foot on (Acts 7:5). We may learn this from the Old Testament record, because we are told that he had to buy from the Canaanites, whom God had promised to drive out, a spot of land in which to bury his wife. As for his immediate descendants, we know that they dwelt in tents, wandering from place to place, and that Jacob died in the land of Egypt.

Further than this, we read the words of David, whose reign was at the time of the highest prosperity of the children of Israel in the land of Canaan: "Hear my prayer, O Lord, and give ear unto my cry; hold not thy peace at my tears; for I am a stranger with thee, and a sojourner, as all my fathers were" (Psalm 39:12). See also his prayer at the consecration of the gifts to the temple, when Solomon was made king (1 Chronicles 29:15).

Still further, and this is most positive of all, we have the words of God to Abraham when He made the promise. After telling him that He would give the land of Canaan to him and to his seed, the Lord said that his seed should first be slaves in a strange land. "And thou shalt go to thy fathers in peace; thou shalt be buried in a good old age. But in the fourth generation they shall come hither again" (Genesis 15:7, 13–16). Thus we see that Abraham was plainly told that he should die before he had any inheritance in the land, and that it would be at least four hundred years before any of his seed could inherit it.

But Abraham died in faith, and so did his seed. See Hebrews 11:13. "These all died in faith, not having received the promises, but having seen them afar off, and were persuaded of them, and embraced them, and confessed that they were strangers and pilgrims on the earth." They died in faith, because they knew that God could not lie. But since God's promise must be fulfilled, and they did not receive the promised inheritance in this present life, we are shut up to the conclusion that it can be obtained only through the resurrection from the dead.

This was the hope that sustained the faithful Israelites. Abraham had faith to offer Isaac upon the altar because his faith was in God's power to raise the dead. When Paul was a prisoner on account of "the hope and resurrection of the dead" (Acts 23:6), he said, "And now I stand and am judged for the hope of the promise made of God unto our fathers; unto which promise our twelve tribes, instantly serving God day and night, hope to come." And then, to show the reasonableness of this hope, he asked, "Why should it be thought a thing incredible with you, that God should raise the dead?" (Acts 26:6–8).

The resurrection of Jesus Christ is the pledge and surety of the resurrection of those who believe on Him. See 1 Corinthians 15:13–20. The apostles "preached through Jesus the resurrection from the dead" (Acts 4:2). And one of them says for our benefit, "Blessed be the God and Father of our Lord Jesus Christ, which according to his abundant mercy hath begotten us again unto a lively hope by the resurrection of Jesus Christ from the dead, to an inheritance incorruptible, and undefiled, and that fadeth not away, reserved in heaven for you, who are kept by the power of God through faith unto salvation ready to be revealed in the last time" (1 Peter 1:3–5).[2]

And then he adds that this faith is tried that it may "be found unto praise and honor and glory at the appearing of Jesus Christ." And this brings us to the conclusion of the matter, namely, that the promise to Abraham and to his seed that they should be heirs of the world, is the promise of Christ's second coming.

The apostle Peter says it is necessary to remind us of the words spoken by the holy prophets because "there shall come in the last days scoffers, walking after their own lusts, and saying, Where is the promise of his coming? for since the fathers fell asleep, all things continue as they were from the beginning of the creation." Therefore they do not believe in the promise at all.

But they do not reason well, "for this they willingly are ignorant of, that by the word of God the heavens were of old, and the earth standing out of the water and in the water, whereby the world that then was being overflowed with water, perished; but the heavens and the earth, which are now, by the same word are kept in store, reserved unto fire against the day of judgment and perdition of ungodly men" (2 Peter 3:5–7).

Take notice that not only has the promise something to do with the fathers, but it concerns the whole earth. The complaint of the scoffers is that since the fathers fell asleep all things continue as they were from the beginning of the creation. But the apostle shows when they say so they shut their eyes to the fact that the same word which in the beginning made the heavens and the earth, also destroyed the earth by the flood. The earth is by the same word now preserved until the day of judgment and perdition of ungodly men, when it will be destroyed by fire. "Nevertheless we, according to His promise, look for new heavens and a new earth, wherein dwelleth righteousness" (2 Peter 3:13).

According to what promise?—Why, according to the promise to the fathers, which was that Abraham and his seed should inherit the earth. It has been a long time, as men count, since that promise was made, but "the Lord is not slack concerning His promise." It has not been so long since it was made that God has forgotten it; for "one day is with the Lord as a thousand years, and a thousand years as one day." The reason

---

2. Waggoner, *Present Truth* UK edition, September 20, 1894.

why He has waited this long is that He is not willing any should perish in the fires that will renew the earth. He desires that all should come to repentance.

And so we find we have as great an interest in the promise to Abraham as he himself had. The promise is still open for all to receive. It embraces nothing less than an eternal life of righteousness in the earth made new as it was in the beginning. The hope of the promise of God unto the fathers was the hope of the coming of the Lord to raise the dead, and thus to bestow the inheritance.

When Christ was once here on the earth He did not have any more of the inheritance than did Abraham. He had not where to lay His head. God is now sending His Holy Spirit to seal the believers for the inheritance, even as He did to Abraham; and when all the faithful shall have been sealed by the Spirit, "He shall send Jesus Christ, which before was preached unto you; whom the heaven must receive until the times of restitution of all things, which God hath spoken by the mouth of all His holy prophets since the world began" (Acts 3:20, 21).

We have learned what Abraham found, and how he found it. At the same time we have learned what God has promised us as well as Abraham, if we believe His word. God has promised to every person who believes Him nothing less than the free possession of the entire world. This is not an arbitrary thing. God has not said that if we will believe certain statements and dogmas, He will in return give us an everlasting inheritance. The inheritance is one of righteousness. Since faith means the reception of the life of Christ into the heart, together with God's righteousness, it is evident there is no other way in which the inheritance can be received. This is further made clear by a statement in the last section, which was not noted, that "the law worketh wrath."

Therefore, whoever thinks to get righteousness by the law is putting his trust in that which will destroy him. God has promised a grant of land to every one who will receive it on His conditions, namely, that he shall also receive the righteousness which goes with it, for righteousness is the characteristic of the land. Righteousness is to "dwell" in it. But this righteousness can be found only in the life of God, which is manifested in Christ.

Now the man who thinks that he himself can get righteousness out of the law is in reality trying to substitute his own righteousness for God's righteousness. In other words, he is trying to get the land by fraud. Therefore, when he comes in the court to prove his claim to the land, it appears there is a criminal charge against him; and he finds "wrath" instead of blessing. "Where no law is, there is no transgression;" but there is law everywhere, and therefore transgression. All have sinned, so that the inheritance can not be by the law.[3]

The Great Joy of Believing the Promise, Romans 4:16–25

Therefore it is of faith, that it might be by grace; to the end the promise might be sure to all the seed; not to that only which is of the law, but to that also which is of the faith of Abraham, who is the father of us all (as it is written, I have made thee a father of many nations), before Him whom he believed, even God, who quickeneth the dead, and calleth those things which be not as though they were. Who against hope believed in hope, that he might become the father of many nations, according to that which was spoken, So shall thy seed be. And being not weak in faith, he considered not his own body now dead, when he was about an hundred years old, neither yet the deadness of Sarah's womb; he staggered not at the promise of God through unbelief; but was strong in faith, giving glory to God; and being fully persuaded, that what He had promised, He was able also to perform. And therefore it was imputed to him for righteousness. Now it was not written for his sake alone, that it was imputed to him; but for us also, to whom it shall be imputed, if we believe on Him that raised up Jesus our Lord from the dead; who was delivered for our offenses, and was raised again for our justification.

Since the inheritance is through the righteousness of faith, it is equally sure to all the seed, and equally within the reach of all. Faith gives all an equal chance, because faith is just as easy for one person as for another. God has dealt to every man a measure of faith, and to all the same measure, for the measure of grace is the measure of faith, and "unto every one of us is given grace according to the measure of the gift of Christ" (Ephesians 4:7). Christ is given without reserve to every person (Hebrews 2:9). Therefore, as the same measure of faith and grace is given to all people, all have an equal opportunity to gain the inheritance.

Faith makes the promise sure to all the seed, because it has Christ alone for its object, and He is the surety of the promises of God (2 Corinthians 1:20). We read also of the oath of God, by which Jesus was made high

---

3. Here is a reference to the *mere right* of possession we studied in a previous chapter. We see that on our own we cannot make claim to the land. Only in Christ is the "mere right" of ownership corrected to an absolute and honest possession.

priest, that "by so much was Jesus made a surety of a better testament," or covenant (Hebrews 7:22). Now Jesus was not given for a certain class, but for all without distinction. "God so loved the world, that He gave His only-begotten Son, that whosoever believeth in Him should not perish, but have everlasting life" (John 3:16). Jesus by the grace of God tasted death for every man (Hebrews 2:9). He says, "Him that cometh to Me I will in no wise cast out" (John 6:37). Christ dwells in the heart by faith (Ephesians 3:17). Therefore, since Christ is the surety of the promise, it must be sure to every one who believes.

It may seem to some a little far-fetched to say that the oath by which Jesus was made priest is the surety of the promise to Abraham. But a little consideration will enable any one to see that it can be no other way. In the sixth chapter of Hebrews we read:—

> For when God made promise to Abraham, because He could swear by no greater, He sware by Himself, saying, Surely blessing I will bless thee, and multiplying I will multiply thee. And so, after he had patiently endured, he obtained the promise. For men verily swear by the greater: and an oath for confirmation is to them an end of all strife. Wherein God, willing more abundantly to shew unto the heirs of promise the immutability of His counsel, confirmed it by an oath: that by two immutable things, in which it was impossible for God to lie, we might have a strong consolation, who have fled for refuge to lay hold upon the hope set before us: which hope we have as an anchor of the soul, both sure and stedfast, and which entereth into that within the veil; wither the forerunner is for us entered, even Jesus, made an high priest for ever after the order of Melchisedec (Hebrews 6:13–20).

Why did God confirm His promise to Abraham by an oath? That we might have a strong consolation. It was not for Abraham's sake, because Abraham believed fully without the oath. His faith was shown to be perfect before the oath was given. It was altogether for our sakes.

When does that oath give us strong consolation? When we flee for refuge to Christ as priest in the most holy place. Within the veil He ministers as high priest; and it is the oath of God that gives us courage to believe that His priesthood will save us. Then our consolation comes from Christ's priesthood, and so from the oath which made Him priest.

Therefore the oath of God to Abraham was identical with the oath that made Christ high priest. This shows most plainly that the promise of God to Abraham is as wide as the gospel of Christ. And so our text, speaking of the righteousness that was imputed to Abraham, says, "Now it was not written for his sake alone, that it was imputed to him; but for us also, to whom it shall be imputed, if we believe on Him that raised up Jesus our Lord from the dead."

God "calleth those things which be not as though they were." Sometimes men do the same thing, but we soon lose confidence in them. When men speak of things that are not as though they were, there is only one proper name for it. It is a lie. But God calls those things that be not as though they were, and it is the truth. What makes the difference? Simply this: Man's word has no power to make a thing exist when it does not exist. He may say that it does, but that does not make it so. But when God names a thing, the very thing itself is in the word that names it. He speaks, and it is. It was by this power of God that Abraham was made the father of many nations, even of us, if we believe that Jesus died and rose again.[4]

Our Birthright to the Inheritance— Christ's Righteousness

"By faith Abraham, when he was called to go out into a place which he should after receive for an inheritance, obeyed; and he went out, not knowing whither he went. By faith he sojourned in the land of promise as in a strange country, dwelling in tabernacles with Isaac and Jacob, the heirs with him of the same promise; for he looked for a city which hath foundations, whose builder and maker is God. Through faith also Sara herself received strength to conceive seed, and was delivered of a child when she was past age, because she judged Him faithful who had promised. Therefore sprang there even of one, and him as good as dead, so many as the stars of the sky in multitude, and as the sand which is by the sea shore innumerable. These all died in faith, not having received the promises, but having seen them afar off, and were persuaded of them, and embraced them, and confessed that they were strangers and pilgrims on the earth. For they that say such things declare plainly that they seek a country. And truly, if they had been mindful of that country from whence they came out, they might have had opportunity to have returned. But now they desire a better country, that is, an heavenly; wherefore God is not ashamed to be called their God; for He hath prepared for them a city." Hebrews 11:8-16.

---

4. E.J. Waggoner, *Romans: The Greatest Treatise Ever Written* (Gordonsville, TN, CFI Book Division, 2019, pp. 90-93).

The first thing that we note in this scripture is that all these were heirs. We have already learned that Abraham himself was to be no more than an heir in this present lifetime, because he was to die before his seed returned from captivity. But Isaac and Jacob, his immediate descendants, were likewise heirs. The children were heirs with their father of the same promised inheritance.[5]

Not only this, but there sprang from Abraham "so many as the stars of the sky in multitude, and as the sand which is by the sea shore innumerable." These were also heirs of the same promise, for these also "all died in faith, not having received the promises, but having seen them afar off, and were persuaded of them, and embraced them, and confessed that they were strangers and pilgrims on the earth." Mark this, the vast host of Abraham's descendants; "died in faith, not having received the promises." Note that it says "promises." It was not simply a part that they did not receive, but the whole. Because all the promises are in Christ only, who is the seed, and they could not be fulfilled to those who are His before they are to Him; and even He yet waits for His foes to be made His footstool.[6]

In harmony with these words, that they died in faith, not having received the promises, but confessed that they were strangers and pilgrims on the earth, we have the words of King David hundreds of years after the deliverance from Egypt, "I am a stranger with Thee, and a sojourner, as all my fathers were" (Psalm 39:12). And when at the height of his power he delivered the kingdom to his son Solomon, in the presence of all the people, he said, "For we are strangers before Thee, and sojourners, as were all our fathers; our days on the earth are as a shadow, and there is none abiding" (1 Chronicles 29:15).

The reason why this innumerable company did not receive the promised inheritance, is stated in these words: "God having provided some better thing for us, that they without us should not be made perfect." The further particulars will be considered when we come to their times.

Abraham looked for a city which hath foundations whose builder and maker is God. The city with foundations is described in Revelation 21:10–14, 19: "And he carried me away in the Spirit to a great and high mountain, and showed me that great city, the holy Jerusalem, descending out of heaven from God, having the glory of God; and her light was like

---

5. E.J. Waggoner, *Present Truth*, July 23, 1896, United Kingdom, p. 465.
6. Ibid.

unto a stone most precious, even like a jasper stone, clear as crystal; and had a wall great and high, and had twelve gates, and at the gates twelve angels, and names written thereon; which are the names of the twelve tribes of the children of Israel; on the east three gates; on the north three gates, on the south three gates; and on the west three gates. And the wall of the city had twelve foundations, and in them the names of the twelve apostles of the Lamb." "And the foundations of the wall of the city were garnished with all manner of precious stones."

That is a partial description of the city for which Abraham looked. His descendants also looked for the same city, for we read descriptions of it in the ancient prophets. They might have had a home on this earth, if they had desired. The land of the Chaldees was as fertile as the land of Palestine, and it would have sufficed for a temporal home for them as well as any other land. But neither one would satisfy them, for "now they desire a better country, that is an heavenly; wherefore God is not ashamed to be called their God; for He hath prepared for them a city."

This scripture kept in mind will guide us in all our subsequent study of the children of Israel. The true children of Abraham never looked for the fulfilment of the promise on this present earth, but in the earth made new.

This desire for a heavenly country made the true heirs very easy to get along with in temporal affairs, as illustrated in the life of Isaac. He went to sojourn in the land of the Philistines, and sowed in that land, "and received in the same year an hundredfold; and the Lord blessed him. And the man waxed great, and went forward, and grew until he became very great; for he had possession of flocks and herds, and great store of servants; and the Philistines envied him ... And Abimelech said unto Isaac, Go from us; for thou art much mightier than we. And Isaac departed thence, and pitched his tent in the valley of Gerar, and dwelt there." Genesis 26:12–17.

Although Isaac was mightier than the people in whose land he dwelt, he went from them at their request, even when he was prospering abundantly. He would not strive for the possession of an earthly estate.

The same spirit was manifested after he went to dwell in Gerar. The servants of Isaac dug anew the wells that had belonged to Abraham, and also dug in the valley and found living water. But the herdmen of Gerar strove with them, saying, "The water is ours." So they went and dug another well; but the herdmen of Gerar claimed that also. "And he removed from thence, and digged another well; and for that they strove not; and he called the name of it Rehoboth; and he said, "For now the

LORD hath made room for us, and we shall be fruitful in the land." (Read Genesis 26:18-22).

"And the LORD appeared to him the same night, and said, I am the God of Abraham thy father; fear not, for I am with thee, and will bless thee, and multiply thy seed for My servant Abraham's sake. And he builded an altar there, and called upon the name of the LORD, and pitched his tent there." (verses 24, 25).

Isaac had the promise of a better country, that is, an heavenly, and therefore he would not strive for the possession of a few square miles of land on this sin-cursed earth. Why should he? It was not the inheritance that the Lord had promised him; and why should he fight for a part in the land wherein he was only a sojourner? True, he had to live, but he allowed the Lord to manage that for him. When driven from one place, he went to another, until at last he found quiet, and then he said, "The LORD hath made room for us." In this he showed the true spirit of Christ, "who, when He was reviled, reviled not again; when He suffered, He threatened not; but committed Himself (His cause) to Him that judgeth righteously" (1 Peter 2:23).

In this we have an example. If we are Christ's, then are we Abraham's seed, and heirs according to the promise. Therefore we shall do the works of Christ. The words of Christ, "I say unto you, That ye resist not evil; but whosoever shall smite thee on thy right cheek, turn to him the other also. And if any man will sue thee at the law,[7] and take away thy coat, let him have thy cloak also" (Matthew 5:39, 40), are thought by many professed Christians to be fanciful, and altogether impractical. But they are designed for daily use. Christ practiced them, and we have an example also in the case of Isaac.

"But we should lose everything that we have in the world, if we should do as the text says," we hear it said. Well, even then we should be in no worse circumstances than Christ the Lord was here on earth. But we are to remember that "your heavenly Father knoweth that ye

---

7. Waggoner included a note for this comment and we reproduce it here. "The thoughtful reader will see in this an exhortation to avoid lawsuits. If one would sue you for your coat, it is better to settle it by giving him both your coat and your cloak than to go to law. This is practical wisdom. Lawsuits are like lotteries; a great deal of money is spent on them, and very little gained. Of course it will be said, 'If we don't defend our rights people will take away everything we have.' And so it would be if God had no care for His people. But defending one's rights does not by any means always preserve them, as many a man has proved to his cost."

have need of all these things." He who cares for the sparrows, is able to care for those who commit their case to Him. We see that Isaac was prospered even though he did not "fight for his rights." The promise which was made to them, is also made to us, by the very same God. "When they were but a few men in number; yea, very few, and strangers" in the land; "when they went from one nation to another, and from one kingdom to another people, He suffered no man to do them wrong; yea, He reproved kings for their sakes; saying, Touch not Mine anointed, and do My prophets no harm" (Psalm 105:12–15). That same God still cares for those who put their trust in Him.

The inheritance which the Lord has promised to His people, the seed of Abraham, is not to be obtained by fighting, except with spiritual weapons,—the armor of Christ,—against the hosts of Satan. They who seek the country which God has promised, declare that they are strangers and pilgrims on this earth. They cannot use the sword, even in self-defence, much less for conquest. The Lord is their defender. He says: "Cursed be the man that trusteth in man, and maketh flesh his arm, and whose heart departeth from the LORD. For he shall be like the heath in the desert, and shall not see when good cometh; but shall inhabit the parched places in the wilderness, in a salt land, and not inhabited. Blessed is the man that trusteth in the LORD, and whose hope the LORD is. For he shall be as a tree planted by the waters, that spreadeth out her roots by the river, and shall not see when heat cometh, but her leaf shall be green" (Jeremiah 17:5–8). He has not promised that all our wrongs shall be righted at once, or even in this life; but He doth not forget the way of the poor, and He has said, Vengeance is Mine; I will repay" (Romans 12:19). Therefore "let them that suffer according to the will of God commit the keeping of their souls to Him in well-doing, as unto a faithful Creator" (1 Peter 4:19). We may do this in full confidence that "the LORD will maintain the cause of the afflicted, and the right of the poor" (Psalm 140:12).

The case of Esau furnishes another incidental proof that the inheritance promised to Abraham and his seed was not a temporal one, to be enjoyed in this life, but eternal, to be shared in the life to come. The story is told in these words:—

> And Jacob sod pottage; and Esau came from the field, and he was faint: and Esau said to Jacob, Feed me, I pray thee, with that same red pottage; for I am faint; therefore was his name called Edom. And Jacob said, Sell me this day thy birthright. And Esau said, Behold, I am at the point to die; and what profit

shall this birthright do me? And Jacob said, Swear to me this day; and he sware unto him; and he sold his birthright unto Jacob. Then Jacob gave Esau bread and pottage of lentils; and he did eat and drink, and rose up, and went his way; thus Esau despised his birthright (Genesis 25:29–34).

In the Epistle to the Hebrews Esau is called a "profane person," because he sold his birthright. This shows that there was something besides mere foolishness in the transaction. One would say that it was childish to sell a birthright for a meal of victuals; but it was worse than childish; it was wicked. It showed that he was an infidel, feeling nothing but contempt for the promise of God to his father.[8]

Notice these words of Esau, when Jacob asked him to sell his birthright: "Behold, I am at the point to die; and what profit shall this birthright do me?" He had no hope beyond this present life, and looked no further. He did not feel sure of anything that he did not actually possess in this present time. No doubt he was very hungry. It is probable that he felt as if he were really at the point of death; but even the prospect of death made no difference with Abraham and many others. They died in faith, not having received the promises, but were persuaded of them, and embraced them. Esau, however had no such faith. He had no belief in an inheritance beyond the grave. Whatever he was to have he wanted now. Thus it was that he sold his birthright.

The course of Jacob is not by any means to be commended. He acted the part of a supplanter, which was his natural disposition. His case is an illustration of a crude, unintelligent faith. He believed that there was something to the promise of God, and he respected his father's faith, although as yet he really possessed none of it. He believed that the inheritance promised to his fathers would be bestowed, but he had so little spiritual knowledge that he supposed the gift of God might be purchased with money. We know that when Abraham thought at one time that he himself must fulfil the promise of God. So Jacob doubtless

---

8. The story of Esau is a life illustration that shows contempt for the everlasting covenant which was the only means of his salvation from sin. Esau scorned and threw away his birthright possession for a mess of pottage to satisfy his immediate physical need. We can do the same if we reject and neglect God's promise to save us *from* sin (Matthew 1:21) by insisting that we cannot resist the immediate and long-term pleasures of sinful living, or by attempting to replace God's promise to save us with our own promises to obey. By either means we are in effect rejecting God's gift of our birthright possession of eternal life in the new earth.

thought, as many do still, that "God helps those who help themselves." Afterwards he learned better, and was truly converted, and exercised as sincere faith as Abraham and Isaac. His case should be an encouragement to us, in that it shows what God can do with one who has a very unlovely disposition, provided he yields to Him.

The case of Esau is set forth before us as a warning. The apostle writes:—

> Follow peace with all men, and holiness, without which no man shall see the Lord; looking diligently lest any man fail of the grace of God; lest any root of bitterness springing up trouble you, and thereby many be defiled; lest there be any fornicator, or profane person, as Esau, who for one morsel of meat sold his birthright. For ye know how that afterward, when he would have inherited the blessing, he was rejected; for he found no place of repentance, though he sought it carefully with tears (Hebrews 12:14–17).

Esau was not the only foolish and profane person there has been in the world. Thousands have done the same thing that he did, even while blaming him for his folly. The Lord has called us all to share the glory of the inheritance which he promised to Abraham. By the resurrection of Jesus Christ from the dead He has begotten us again to a living hope, "to an inheritance incorruptible, undefiled, and that fadeth not away, reserved in heaven for you who are kept by the power of God through faith unto salvation ready to be revealed in the last time" (1 Peter 1:3–5). This inheritance of righteousness we are to have through the obedience of faith,—obedience to God's holy law, the ten commandments. But when they learn that it requires the observance of the seventh day, the Sabbath kept by Abraham, Isaac, and Jacob, and all Israel, they shake their heads. "No," say they, "I cannot do that; I should like to, and I see that it is a duty; but if I should keep it I could not make a living. I should be thrown out of employment, and should starve together with my family."

That is just the way Esau reasoned. He was about to starve, or at least, he thought that he was, and so he deliberately parted with his birthright for something to eat. But most men do not even wait until they are apparently at the point of death, before they sell their right to the inheritance, for something to eat. Men do not often starve to death for serving the Lord. We are entirely dependent upon Him for our life under all circumstances, and if He keeps us when we are trampling on His law, He surely is as able to keep us when we are serving Him. The

Saviour says that to worry over the future, fearing lest we should starve, is a characteristic of heathenism, and gives us this positive assurance, "Seek ye first the kingdom of God, and His righteousness, and all these things shall be added unto you" (Matthew 6:21-33). The Psalmist says, I have been young, and now am old; yet have I not seen the righteous forsaken, nor his seed begging bread." Even though we should lose our lives for the sake of the truth of God, we should be in good company. (See Hebrews 11:32–38). Let us beware of so lightly esteeming the rich promises of God that we shall part with an eternal inheritance for a morsel of bread, and when it is too late find that there is no place for repentance.[9]

9. Waggoner, *The Everlasting Covenant*, pp. 97-105.

Part IX

Persistence
of
Old Covenant Thinking

29

An Illustration of the Tenaciousness of the Old Covenant Attitude

A hard heart is the root of unbelief and is the source of our continued rebellion against God. Just as it is Laodicea's problem, a hard heart had been Pharaoh's problem, too. Pharaoh's attitude toward God's attempts to reorient his thinking is an illustration of everyone's problem, even today. What was the lesson God intended for Pharaoh and all of Egypt to learn? "And the Egyptians shall know that I am the LORD" (Exodus 7:5). It was the very same lesson God was attempting to teach the children of Israel (Exodus 16:12; 29:46). He is trying to teach us the same thing today. How did God go about teaching Pharaoh and the Egyptians? "When I stretch forth Mine hand upon Egypt, and bring out the children of Israel from among them," then they will know that Jehovah is LORD over all the earth. Through their persistent rebellion, the Egyptians needlessly brought upon themselves plagues and losses God never intended them to suffer.

Before the seventh plague, Moses stood before Pharaoh again, this time entreating Pharaoh to heed the warning of the coming plague. "Send therefore now, and gather thy cattle, and all that thou hast in the field; for upon every man and beast which shall be found in the field, the hail shall come down upon them, and they shall die" (Exodus 10:19). Pharaoh stubbornly disbelieved the evidence, even though Moses had been right in his calamitous predictions six out of six times. Now, God through Moses is inviting anyone who will believe "in the word of the LORD" to spare themselves pain and loss by bringing under shelter all livestock and people. Did they listen? The next two verses tell the tale. "He that feared the word of the LORD among the servants of Pharaoh made his servants and his cattle flee into the houses: and he that regarded not the word of the LORD left his servants and cattle in the field" (vss. 20, 21).

Pharaoh's main problem was that he considered himself on equal terms with this God of the Israelites. He told Moses, "Who is the LORD that I should obey His voice?" (Exodus 5:2). When Pharaoh asked Moses, Who is this God that I should listen to Him, he was not denying that God was a god, he was denying that God is the *supreme* God of all the universe. Pharaoh had no problem accepting the presence of one more deity. The pantheon of Egypt was large, but Pharaoh was "god" over all. Who was *this* God that Pharaoh had never before known, who now came demanding he should bow down to Him? Pharaoh was in essence stating that the God of Moses assumed to be greater than himself, and he refused to accept that idea as truth.

The ten plagues were a showdown between Pharaoh, who believed he was god over all, and the one true God of the universe. Because Pharaoh was accepted in Egypt as god over all of nature, God struck those things in nature worshipped by the Egyptians which Pharaoh claimed to control. That's why the plagues involved things sacred to the Egyptians. Through these demonstrations of power over nature Jehovah proved He was LORD over all of His creation. Pharaoh's persistent refusal to accept this fact hardened his heart as he dug in his heels, bracing himself against the truth. Israel "could have escaped from Egypt during any one of the Ten Plagues, while Egypt was trapped in its suffering, and G-d could have continued the plagues until Israel reached the Promised Land or even forever. But Hashem desired more than this, that Pharaoh should also answer Amen; to admit that everyone must accept the Will of the Creator, even Egyptian kings."[1]

Pharaoh's arrogant, self-centered pride was the root of his rebellion. "When G-d first sent Moses to Pharaoh, all he asked for was to let Israel out for three days. Moshe however, did not say, 'Let my people go,' as in the King James Version. He demanded one thing more: 'Send out my people;' you, Pharaoh, *must* send them out; you, too, *must* agree to do the Will of Hashem."[2]

It took four plagues before Pharaoh relented and conceded that the Israelites "could sacrifice to [their] God in the land"—not out in the wilderness, but in Egypt (Exodus 8:25). Moses refused this concession, demanding they be allowed to go into the wilderness (vs. 26-27). Pharaoh acted deceitfully, never really intending to let his property get out of his

---

1. Rabbi Yisroel Miller, "The Pharaoh Fantasy," *What's Wrong with Being Happy?* (Brooklyn, NY: Mesorah Publications, 1994), p. 96.
2. Ibid., p. 96; emphasis in original.

hands. All he wanted was an end of the plague. He was sorry for the things he was suffering, but not sorry enough to repent and agree that God was Sovereign LORD of all the earth.

Five more plagues came and went, this time affecting only the Egyptians. Pharaoh called Moses again, finally commanding Moses and all the Israelites to "go out" to worship their God. However, Pharaoh still had a stipulation. The people could go, but they couldn't take their livestock with them. Most people assume that Pharaoh made this stipulation as a guarantee the Israelites would return to their possessions when their worship services were completed, but this overlooks the facts.

> Once we recognize the dynamics of the relationship between Moses and Pharaoh, we can understand Pharaoh's offer to let Israel go if their animals stayed, and why Moses countered by insisting that Pharaoh himself must contribute animals. Since keeping the Jewish cows would not make the slaves return to bondage, why was it so important to Pharaoh that they remain behind? The answer is that it was a symbol. If Pharaoh can keep something, anything at all, even a cow, he will then be able to say (at least to himself): "I and the Jewish G-d made a deal, we negotiated as equals; I gave him the people, and I took the cattle." But if Pharaoh can say that, he negates the whole point of the Ten Plagues, which is that God's Will is all there is. Moshe therefore had to make the point by now demanding more cattle, that Pharaoh must also give offerings to demonstrate that God alone is the Sovereign, and with the Sovereign one does not make deals.[3]

E.J. Waggoner made it clear that Pharaoh's attitude is with us still.

> Many [people] think that Christ is a valuable adjunct, a good Assistant to their efforts. Others are willing to give Him first place, but not the only place. They regard themselves as good seconds. It is the Lord *and they* who do the work. ... That which makes all the trouble is that even when men are willing to recognize the LORD at all they want to make bargains with Him. They want it to be an equal, "mutual" affair—a transaction in which they can consider themselves on a par with God. But whoever deals with God must deal with Him on His own

---

3. Ibid., p. 97.

terms, that is, on a basis of fact—that we have nothing and are nothing, and He has everything and is everything and gives everything.[4]

It is vital to correctly understand the issue. The controversy is over the *way* of salvation, whether by Christ alone, or by something else. As Waggoner stated, many people imagine they must save themselves by making themselves "good" and therefore worthy of God's promises. Others think Christ is a valuable accessory, a good associate to their efforts. Some may be willing to give Christ the first place, but not the only place in their lives, thinking that they can occupy a close second in the deal. Like Pharaoh, they regard themselves as co-regents in the rule of their lives. Their opinion is as valid as God's will and whatever seems "right" to them must at least be considered as an option. This is fantasy from beginning to end.

> Righteousness, whether to men, to angels, to bright seraphim, or to exalted cherubim, comes not by obedience of their own, from their own "promise" under a "compact," upon "condition" and proviso. It comes only from the grace of God through the faith of Jesus Christ; never their own righteousness which is of the law, but always only "that which is through the faith of Christ, the righteousness which is of God by faith" (Philippians 3:9).
>
> And in this word "faith" I mean not a mere theoretical notion, but "faith" in its only true meaning of the *will submitted* to Him, the *heart yielded* to Him, and the *affections fixed* upon Him. This only is faith; and this itself by the grace and gift of God. And this faith, of the will submitted *to* God through Christ, of the heart yielded to God *in* Christ, and the affections fixed upon God *by* Christ—this is the faith of angels as truly as of men.[5]

Can we make a bargain with the Monarch of the universe? Can we consider ourselves on par with God? What have we to offer the Lord in our transaction in the promise of salvation? We have our sins, our

---

4. Waggoner, *The Glad Tidings*, pp. 69 and 71.

5. A.T. Jones, *The Everlasting Gospel of the Everlasting Covenant*, pp.16, 17, 19; a self published document, from remarks Jones made in the Battle Creek Sanitarium Sabbath School on July 20, 1907 (emphases in original). In this document Jones addresses the persistent old covenantism present in the 1907 General Conference *Adult Sabbath School Quarterly*. The last paragraph defines faithful allegiance to God—"the will submitted … the heart yielded … the affections fixed."

unrighteousness, and our eternal inheritance of the grave. In our natural selves, we possess no goodness, no righteousness and no promise of eternal life. In short, we are nothing, we have nothing, and we have nothing to give.

What does God bring to the bargaining table? All the things we lack. He is everything, He has everything, and He gives everything. After demonstrating His awesome power in humiliating Pharaoh, proving beyond any doubt that all the things the Egyptians worshipped were without strength, God brought the Israelites out into the desert where they could learn the same lesson: they were without strength and needed Him as their Redeemer and Sustainer. This was the message God attempted to give to the unbelieving Israelites during their forty-year wilderness sojourn. He wanted them to believe the covenant He had previously given to Abraham, Isaac and Jacob, the covenant based on faith in God's power to deliver what He promised.

God promised Abraham he would inherit the world. God did not make this promise to Abraham "through the law" but through faith (see Romans 4:13). In Genesis 17 we read that God made a covenant with Abraham to give him the land of Canaan for an *everlasting* possession. Galatians 3:18 says that God gave it to Abraham by promise. Therefore, we can conclude that God's covenants and His promises are one and the same thing. *That* promise, *that* oath which God made to Abraham is our ground of hope, our "strong consolation" (Hebrews 6:18). The promise to Abraham was to every human being.

> There is neither Jew nor Greek, there is neither bond nor free, there is neither male nor female: for ye are all one in Christ Jesus. And if ye be Christ's, then are ye Abraham's seed, and heirs according to the promise (Galatians 3:28, 29).

God pledged His very own existence, and with it the entire universe, for our salvation from sin (Matthew 1:21; Hebrews 2:9). If God cannot fulfill His promise, then He doesn't deserve to be God. Satan will be proven to have made a valid accusation against the Creator and Sovereign of the universe. God's promise to Abraham included a conveyance of land in which he could live eternally. God has promised a grant of land to all who will receive it on His conditions. Since only righteousness will dwell in the new earth, God's promise includes the gift of righteousness to all who believe.[6]

---

6. See *The Glad Tidings*, p. 72.

Anyone who thinks he can get righteousness by keeping the law in his own strength is in reality trying to substitute his own unrighteousness for God's righteousness. In other words, he is trying to obtain the promised possession by fraudulent dealing. God's covenants can be nothing other than God's promises. God has promised His people, regardless of their ethnic background, an everlasting possession wherein dwelleth righteousness (see 2 Peter 3:7, 11–13).

This is the sum total of the Gospel. "The free gift of God is eternal life in Jesus Christ our Lord" (Romans 6:23). This gift of eternal life is included in the gift of Christ's righteousness and with that, we gain the right to the possession of the new earth. Since only righteousness will inherit the new earth, the promise includes the making righteous of all who believe God's promise. The power by which we are redeemed is the same power which, in the beginning, created the world and by which the heavens and earth will be made new. Is this not glorious good news? How can we doubt that this same creative power will also save us from a life of continual sinning and repenting, sinning and repenting, which nauseates Christ?[7] Believe God's promises to you and you *will* be a Commandment-keeper by the faith of Jesus working in you.

In Galatians 2:16, 20 and Revelation 14:12 many modern translations take the Greek word Χριστου (Christ), which is in the masculine singular genitive case (possesive), and translate it as though it was a dative case word. The genitive ending of the word in this verse tells all. What the apostle Paul wrote was that the faith *belongs to Christ Himself*; it is *His* faith through which we are saved. It is not our personal faith *in Him* that saves us, as translations such as the NIV, ESV, ASV, NRSV, NLT, etc. indicate by saying "in Christ" instead of saying "of Christ."

In contrast to these, it is *His own* faith working *in* and *through* us by the power of the Holy Spirit which transforms our characters into His likeness.

> And such trust have we through Christ to God-ward: not that we are sufficient of ourselves to think any thing as of ourselves; but our sufficiency is of God (2 Corinthians 3:4, 5).

> Abide in Me, and I in you. As the branch cannot bear fruit of itself, except it abide in the vine; no more can ye, except ye abide in Me. I am the vine, ye are the branches: He that abideth in Me, and I in him, the same bringeth forth much fruit: for without Me ye can do nothing (John 15:4, 5).

---

7. Revelation 3:16. Christ says that He is so nauseated by our lukewarm attitude toward His love for us, that it literally makes Him feel like He is ready to vomit.

Wherefore, my beloved, as ye have always obeyed, not as in my presence only, but now much more in my absence, work out your own salvation with fear and trembling. For it is God which worketh in you both to will and to do of His good pleasure. Do all things without murmurings and disputings: that ye may be blameless and harmless, the sons of God, without rebuke, in the midst of a crooked and perverse nation, among whom ye shine as lights in the world; holding forth the word of life; that I may rejoice in the day of Christ, that I have not run in vain, neither laboured in vain (Philippians 2:12–16).

Every good gift and every perfect gift is from above, and cometh down from the Father of lights, with Whom is no variableness, neither shadow of turning (James 1:17).

This gift of *His* faith to us is a fundamental concept of the Gospel's message. God has "dealt to every man the measure of faith"—not *a* measure, but *the* measure. *The* "measure" is Christ and His righteousness in its fullness.

Changing the Greek to the dative case implies we have some part to play in the salvation process. It suggests that by exercising my personal faith, by trying hard enough to believe, then by my efforts I am contributing a part to my salvation. Therefore, faith becomes a work we must do in order to gain merit to be saved, like the often seen signs along the roadside seem to tell us: "Just believe on the Lord Jesus Christ, and thou shalt be saved."

This oft quoted fragment takes Paul's statement completely out of context of the Gospel's message to save us *from* sin, not *in* our sins without any transformation of our character. The truth is that salvation is *ALL* from God, we contribute nothing. It is a free gift we may keep and cherish, or waste and throw away.

None of the evangelical or Reformed positions are correct; there are not two dispensations[8] and certainly not two methods of salvation, one under the "Jewish dispensation" effected through the ritual sacrifice of animals, and a second under the "New Testament covenant" of Christ's crucifixion. The apostle Paul said: God "hath chosen us *IN HIM* before the foundation of the world" (Ephesians 1:4, 5, 11). Before there was sin in the world the promise of salvation was a "done deal." When Adam

----

8. There is no such thing as a "Jewish dispensation." There is no referance to the "Jews" being at Sinai. The children of Israel weren't called Jews until after their return from Babylonian captivity.

fell into sin the plan of salvation from sin (the everlasting covenant) had already been established by the eternal Godhead. That plan, made active in the Garden of Eden by promise, was ratified on Calvary's cross by the shed blood of the true Lamb of God.

We were all "predestined" to be children of God from before the foundation of the world. *IN CHRIST*, from the foundation of the world, we were given all blessings which included the promise of inheritance of the earth made new and the righteousness required to obtain it.

The promise God made to Abraham was a covenant based on mutual faith. First, God's faith in Abraham's fidelity to Him as his God, and second, Abraham's willingness to believe God's promise to give him a land and make him a great nation. Abraham's faith is in contrast to the suzerain contract made at Sinai which was not based on faith. At Sinai the people promised, "all that the LORD has spoken we will do," depending on their *own* abilities to fulfill God's promise, rather than acknowledge their impotence and utter inabiltiy to fulfill their promise to God.

These two basic premises have, since antiquity, formed the fundamental elements for the discussions of the Bible's salvation message and are the foundation of the debate: Is salvation accomplished by faith alone in God's promises to save, or by a combination of faith plus works? Faith is considered by many to be a form of works, our "acts" of faith, which implies merit in our own works in the salvation equation.

But the reality of "faith" must be centered on God's work in saving mankind *through* Christ "from the foundation of the world" (Revelation 13:8; 1 Peter 1:18–20; Hebrews 4:3; 1 John 4:14).[9] The instruction to Adam about the tree in the midst of the garden was, "thou shalt not eat of it: for in the day that thou eatest thereof thou shalt *surely die*" (Genesis 2:17).[10] The only reason Adam did not die on the spot, is found in the everlasting covenant of the Godhead to "save His people from their sin" (Matthew 1:21).

The very instant Adam ate the fruit, the everlasting covenant went into effect as Christ stepped between the Living God and "dead" Adam,

---

9. See author's document "What *IS* Legal Justification?"; a brief study on the history of the theology of forensic justification from the time of the Protestant Reformation. (Available on www.gospel-herald.com).

10. The original Hebrew uses a doubling of the word מו·ת (mût) to emphasize that if Adam ate of the tree of knowledge, he would definitely (*surely*) die at that moment. There is no implication in God's declaration that if Adam sinned he would continue to live for a long period of time and eventually die of old age.

placing Adam on a second probation.[11] At that instant the life of Christ was given to allow Adam's life to continue. Christ is truly "the Lamb slain from the foundation of the world." Adam's next heart beat and breath was by the grace of God as Christ, our Surety, immediately assumed accountability and accepted the ultimate consequence of sin that would befall Him 4000 years later when He died on Calvary's cross for the sin of the world (John 1:19; cf. Romans 5:6–10 and 15–21).

As soon as there was sin, there was a Saviour. Christ knew what He would have to suffer, yet He became man's substitute. As soon as Adam sinned, the Son of God presented Himself as surety for the human race, with just as much power to avert the doom pronounced upon the guilty as when He died upon the cross of Calvary.[12]

The instant man accepted the temptations of Satan, and did the very things God had said he should not do, Christ, the Son of God, stood between the living and the dead, saying, 'Let the punishment fall on Me. I will stand in man's place. He shall have another chance.'[13]

The Gospel we have in the New Testament is the same as that which was given to Adam, Noah, and Abraham. The apostle Paul tells us "for unto us was the gospel preached, as well as unto them" (Hebrews 4:1–3; cf. 1 Peter 1:18–20). "Them" points back to those who, under the guidance of Moses came out of Egypt, but who never learned to live by faith. Instead of faith they chose to live by their faltering, earthly vision, falling dead in the wilderness, never seeing the promised land. They could not enter into God's rest for they relied on their own works and disbelieved God's promises (Hebrews 3:8–19).

God is waiting with longing desire for a people who will finally recognize all that He has accomplished for the entire human race "in Christ" through His promise made before the foundation of the world, and revealed to Adam and Eve in Genesis 3:15. When a people learn to appreciate God's everlasting covenant, finally surrender their whole being to Christ, succumbing to His matchless self-emptying love (Philippians 2:5–8), then God will be able to declare, "Here are they that keep the Commandments of God, and the faith of Jesus!" (Revelation 14:12). Then He will come to end this dark night of woe on earth, the

---

11. E.G. White, *Review and Herald*, March 3, 1901.

12. White, *Review and Herald*, March 12, 1901.

13. White, Letter 22, Feb. 13, 1900.

result of Adam's sin, which has blighted human existence for the last 6000 years. Sin will be no more; there will be no more tears or pain. All things will be made new. The promise given to Abraham that he "should inherit the *whole earth*" will come to complete fulfillment.

And I saw a new heaven and a new earth: for the first heaven and the first earth were passed away; and there was no more sea. And I John saw the holy city, new Jerusalem, coming down from God out of heaven, prepared as a bride adorned for her husband. And I heard a great voice out of heaven saying, Behold, the tabernacle of God is with men, and He will dwell with them, and they shall be His people, and God Himself shall be with them, and be their God.

And God shall wipe away all tears from their eyes; and there shall be no more death, neither sorrow, nor crying, neither shall there be any more pain: for the former things are passed away. And He that sat upon the throne said, Behold, I make all things new.

And He said unto me, Write: for these words are true and faithful. And He said unto me, It is done. I am Alpha and Omega, the beginning and the end. I will give unto him that is athirst of the fountain of the water of life freely. He that overcometh shall inherit all things; and I will be his God, and he shall be My son. (Revelation 21:1–7).

For the honor and vindication of God's holy name, pray that this happens soon. Amen.

Bibliography

Alter, Robert: *Genesis, Translation and Commentary*

Beecher, Willis Judson: *The Prophets and the Promise*

Bright, John: *A History of Israel*

Butler, G.I.: *The Law in Galatians*

Clines, David J.A.: *The Theme of the Pentateuch*

de Jong, Peter Y.: *The Covenant Idea in New England Theology*

Dumbrell, William J.: *The Faith of Israel*

Edersheim, Alfred: *Old Testament Bible History*

Eichrodt, Walter: *Theology of the Old Testament, two volumes*

Garner, Bryan, ed.: *Black's Law Dictionary*

Hillers, Delbert R.: *Covenant, The History of a Biblical Idea*

Jones, A.T.: *The Everlasting Gospel in the Everlasting Covenant*

Josephus, Flavius: *The Complete Works of Josephus*

Kaiser, Jr., Walter C.: *Toward an Exegetical Theology*

Kaiser, Jr., Walter C.: *Quest for Renewal*

Kline, Meredith: *The Structure of Biblical Authority*

Kline, Meredith: *Kingdom Prologue*

LaSor, William Sanford, David Allan Hubbard, and Frederic Wm. Bush: *Old Testament Survey*

Lillback, Peter A.: *The Binding of God*

Mendenhall, George E.: *Law and Covenant in Israel and the Ancient Near East*

Miller, Rabbi Yisroel: *What's Wrong with Being Happy?*

Nicholson, Ernest W.: *God and His People*

Pelcovitz, Rabbi Raphael: *Sforno Pentateuch with Commentary*

Postgate, J.N.: *Neo-Assyrian Royal Grants and Decrees*

Pfeiffer, Charles E: *Old Testament History*

Sailhammer, John H.: *The Pentateuch as Narrative*

Sarna, Nahum M.: *Jewish Publication Society Torah Commentary on Genesis*

Sarna, Nahum M.: *JPS Torah Commentary on Exodus*

Scherman, Rabbi Nossen: I *and II Samuel Commentary*

Smith, Ralph Allen: *The Eternal Covenant*

Smith, Ralph Lee: *Old Testament Theology*

Smith, Uriah: "The Two Covenants" (an article)

Waggoner, E.J.: *The Glad Tidings*

Waggoner, E.J.: *Waggoner on Romans*

Waggoner, E.J.: *The Everlasting Covenant*

Waggoner, E.J.: "The Gospel in Galatians" (an article)
Waggoner, E.J.: *Studies in the Book of Hebrews* (General Conference
   Bulletin sermons)
Waggoner, E.J.: *The Gospel in Galatians*
Weinfeld, Moshe: "The Covenant of Grant in the Old Testament and
   in the Ancient Near East," *Journal of the American Oriental Society*
   (1970), pp. 184-203; reprinted in *Essential Papers on Israel and the
   Ancient Near East* (1991).
Wright, N.T.: *Climax of the Covenant, Christ and the Law in
   Pauline Theology*